QM Library

23 1262875 5

KU-256-920

MAIN LIBRARY
QUEEN MARY, UNIVERSITY OF LONDON
Mile End Road, London E1 4NS
DATE DUE FOR RETURN

GENDER DEMOCRACY IN TRADE UNIONS

For Mary Foster

Gender Democracy in Trade Unions

ANNE McBRIDE
University of Warwick

Ashgate

Aldershot • Burlington USA • Singapore • Sydney

© Anne McBride 2001

All rights reserved. No part of this publication may be reproduced, stored in a retrieval system, or transmitted in any form or by any means, electronic, mechanical, photocopying, recording or otherwise without the prior permission of the publisher.

Published by
Ashgate Publishing Limited
Gower House
Croft Road
Aldershot
Hants GU11 3HR
England

Ashgate Publishing Company
131 Main Street
Burlington, VT 05401-5600 USA

Ashgate website: http://www.ashgate.com

British Library Cataloguing in Publication Data
McBride, Anne
    Gender democracy in trade unions
    1. UNISON 2. Women labor union members - Great Britain
    I. Title
    331.8'8'082'0941

Library of Congress Control Number: 2001087935

ISBN 0 7546 1182 5

QUEEN MARY
UNIVERSITY OF LONDON
LIBRARY

Printed in Great Britain by
Antony Rowe Ltd, Chippenham, Wiltshire

Contents

Lists of Figures and Tables

Figures

Tables

Acknowledgements

Many thanks are given to the many members and officers of UNISON who gave so freely of their time and opinions during this study. For reasons of confidentiality it is not possible to name them individually but their generous help and endless patience with my study has been invaluable.

I am indebted to The Economic and Social Research Council who funded the original research and, more indirectly, provided an excellent resource in the form of the Industrial Relations Research Unit, University of Warwick. I am particularly grateful for the valuable support provided by Mike Terry and Linda Dickens. Thanks also to Caroline Lloyd, Sonia Liff, Paul Edwards and Richard Hyman for passing comment on this work at various stages. Comments made by Cynthia Cockburn and John Kelly have been useful in moving towards the final text and I thank them both for their contributions. This text has also benefited from the generous support and technical assistance provided by Val Jephcott. My last set of thanks is to Charlie, Mary, Harry and Jackie who have supported me in every way possible.

List of Abbreviations

AGM	Annual General Meeting
APT&C	Administrative, Professional, Technical and Clerical Staff Group
BEOW	Branch Equality Officer (Women)
CCT	Compulsory Competitive Tendering
CFDU	Campaign for a Fighting Democratic Unison
COHSE	Confederation of Health Service Employees
DSO	Direct Services Organisation
EOC	Equal Opportunities Commission
FTO	Full-time Officer
HC	Health Care
HCSG	Health Care Service Group
HCSGE	Health Care Service Group Executive
LG	Local Government
LGSG	Local Government Service Group
LGSGE	Local Government Service Group Executive
LP	Labour Party
M&C	Manual and Craft
NALGO	National and Local Government Officers' Association
NDC	National Delegate Conference
NEC	National Executive Council
NHS	National Health Service
NLGC	National Lesbian and Gay Committee
NUPE	National Union of Public Employees
NWCf	National Women's Conference
NWCm	National Women's Committee
RHA	Regional Health Authority
SG	Service Group
SGE	Service Group Executive
SOG	Self-organised Group
STV	Single Transferable Vote
SWOMP	Socialist Women on Male Platforms

TUC   Trades Union Congress
TUPE   Transfer of Undertakings (Protection of Employment)
           Regulations 1981

1 Introduction

This book looks at the attempts of the largest British trade union, UNISON, to support equality of representation and participation amongst its female-dominated membership. Whilst democracy infers equality, this is often a desirable rather than a defining feature (Holden, 1993). UNISON's rule book provides structures that guarantee representative equality for its female membership. I have therefore used the concept of 'gender democracy' to indicate that equality between men and women members is a defining feature of UNISON and is the specific focus of this book.

This book has four main aims. First, it describes and analyses UNISON's strategies for reshaping trade union democracy and achieving gender democracy. Secondly, it illustrates the difference this reshaping makes to women's participation and representation. Thirdly, it exposes how these strategies can be blocked and limited. Finally, it argues that union structures need to be organised around principles of individual and group representation. In essence, it argues that UNISON's structures are a necessary element of equality between men and women, but not a sufficient condition for the empowerment of women as a social group.

In itself, noting that equal opportunities policies are necessary but not sufficient is nothing new. What is new is that UNISON is the first British trade union to adopt a comprehensive range of strategies that relate to the representation and participation of individual women and women as a social group. An added feature of this research is the detailed study of the decision-making committees in the union that made it possible to address questions of 'what difference does it make?' Finally, the analysis draws on wider political theory that addresses the redistribution of power to oppressed social groups. This provides a powerful explanation of why UNISON's strategies are not sufficient in themselves to empower women as a social group.

This chapter provides the context and content of the study. The next section gives an overview of the changing face of British trade unionism and provides the context in which UNISON emerged as the largest UK trade union. The chapter identifies essential elements in UNISON's new model of democracy and provides an overview of the research approach. The chapter closes with an outline of the remainder of the book.

The changing face of British trade unionism

Much has been written about the dramatic change in British trade unionism since Margaret Thatcher's Conservative Government came to power in 1979. The first, and foremost change, is the dramatic decline in membership across Britain during the 1980s and 1990s. Over a twenty-year period, membership has fallen by 40 per cent. It now stands at 7.2 million, 30 per cent of all employees (Hicks, 2000). Women make up 44 per cent of the workforce and approximately 40 per cent of trade union members are women. The Trades Union Congress (TUC) – which is the umbrella organisation for 80 per cent of all trade union members – believes that recruiting more women will be a key factor in reversing the decline in membership.

The Workplace Industrial Relations Survey series indicates that the number of workplaces with a trade union presence fell from nearly 75 per cent in 1980 to 50 per cent in 1998, and the number of workplaces recognising trade unions fell from 65 per cent to 42 per cent over the same period (Millward et al., 2000). However, these are aggregate figures and a slightly different picture emerges when these figures are analysed by sector.

The public sector employs approximately one-fifth of the British workforce, 60 per cent of whom are women. Ninety-seven per cent of public sector workplaces retain a trade union presence. This stability compares with a fall of 77 per cent to 42 per cent in private manufacturing and a fall of 50 to 35 per cent in private services in the last two decades. In addition, although the number of public sector workplaces recognising trade unions fell from 94 per cent to 87 per cent over the same period, this was a relatively small fall, primarily explained by the dismantling of the national negotiating system for teachers (Millward et al., 2000). However, if we look at union density at workplace level, it is possible to see the effects of the privatisation of nationalised industries, new management practices and the contracting-out of public services to private sector companies.

Between 1980 and 1998, union density in public sector workplaces fell from 84 per cent to 57 per cent, with the steepest fall taking place from 1990 to 1998. Analysis by Millward et al. shows how workplace changes affected union density. Those workplaces that remained in the public sector retained a relatively stable union density. However, the workplaces which were being privatised were those with the highest density (91 per cent), and the new public sector workplaces being created had a lower aggregate density. In addition, to losing members, Fairbrother (1996) argues that the traditionally centralised and hierarchical public sector unions were unable to deal adequately with the major restructuring and reorganisation within the public sector. Such changes saw a move to individual, rather than uniform, terms and conditions, a shift to local bargaining and a modification of previously consensual bargaining relationships. It is within this context that UNISON was created from the merger of NALGO, NUPE and COHSE.

A 'new' union

The period of dramatic membership decline saw an increase in union mergers, with unions becoming more inclusive in their membership. Britain's two hundred plus unions seek to represent workers in a variety of forms. Although the British trade union movement grew out of the organisation of craft workers, craft-only unions are relatively rare. More common is the industrial or occupational union that restricts its membership to particular occupations or industries or the general union that represents workers across a range of jobs and industries. In 1979, 109 unions were affiliated to the TUC. By 1999, this had fallen to 76 (TUC, 1999). In July 1993, NALGO, NUPE and COHSE merged to become the largest union in Britain and the third largest in Europe.

NALGO, which could be described as a white-collar public service union, predominantly organised clerical and professional officers in local government and the NHS (see Spoor, 1967; Newman, 1982; Miller, 1996). Prior to the merger, NALGO was the largest partner union. It represented approximately 750,000 members, 55 per cent of whom were women. NUPE operated in similar workplaces to NALGO, organising nurses and ancillary staff in the NHS and manual workers in local government (see Dix and Williams, 1987; Fryer et al., 1974 and 1978). It represented approximately 550,000 members, 74 per cent of whom were women. The third union, COHSE, organised nurses and ancillary staff in the NHS (see Carpenter, 1988). It represented approximately 200,000 members, 80 per cent of whom were women. Once merged, UNISON represented almost one million women, approximately half of whom worked part-time. UNISON also represented a significant number of black workers – estimated to be 10 per cent of the membership (Southern and Eastern Regional TUC Women's Rights Committee, 2000).

Although there was a history of rivalry between the unions, by joining together they were more likely to win any competitions that arose for single-union recognition in the restructured public sector organisations (Waddington and Whitston, 1995). The merger also had implications for the structure of the trade union movement. It was anticipated that the merged union would represent one in 18 of all workers in the country, one in six trade unionists and one-third of all women union members (Labour Research, 1993).

Merger discussions started between NALGO and NUPE in 1988, with COHSE joining the talks a year later, cautiously following a 'twin-track' approach to involvement or continued independence (Fryer, 2000). As this study will show, reconciling differences between these three unions had implications for the final structure of UNISON. Chapter 3 describes the partial reconciliation of two significant differences – the employment of paid officers, and equal opportunities strategies. Underpinning these organisational differences is the occupational heterogeneity amongst the membership of the previous unions. UNISON represents a far wider range of workers than the former partner unions. Of particular significance was the amalgamation of all grades of worker in the same union. Reference was made earlier to new management practices that led to job losses in the public sector. Senior management, organised by NALGO, drew up and implemented plans for contracting out the jobs performed by NUPE members (Fryer, 2000). Both sets of workers are now organised within the same union. The union also encompasses workers from NUPE and COHSE who had previously been fierce competitors in the health service (Fryer, 2000).

UNISON can be categorised as an industrial union since its primary area of organisation is in public services – despite successive waves of privatisation ensuring the transfer of services, and workers, to the voluntary and private sectors. Although it is the largest union in the public sector, it is important to note that UNISON does not organise all workers within this sector. More specifically, it organises workers across a range of public service sectors: former utilities of electricity, gas, water; health care; higher education; local government, and transport. Within each sector, members could be further categorised within a number of craft, manual, white-collar and occupational groupings. Through being the largest union in the TUC, UNISON gained more power on the TUC's General Council and many hoped the creation of UNISON would be an exciting opportunity to change radically the structure and purpose of British trade unions (see Terry, 1996).

So what's new?

UNISON has adopted certain principles that have the potential to challenge traditional models of trade unionism. First, it has supported the reservation of seats in proportion to the numbers of women in the constituency. Although there is nothing new in reserved seats, women are the majority of UNISON's membership, so 'this means bringing in considerably more women than previously occupied representative positions. At the same time, it supports self-organisation for women. Again, this is not new in itself, but it is unusual for this to be implemented at the same time as women are set to gain the majority of representative seats. A third strategy has been to provide self-organised groups with rights of representation to mainstream committees.

The next chapter argues that these strategies challenge traditional conceptions of representative democracy. Given the dominance of women in the union, the first strategy necessitates limitations on representation by a specific group, that is, men. The second gives women the potential to use two routes into the democratic process – as an individual and as a member of a social group (Cockburn, 1996). The third gives social groups the same status as individuals. Although some unions have adopted parts of some of these strategies, UNISON has implemented all three at the same time. Two key research questions arise from this model: does UNISON succeed in putting it into practice and what difference does it make to women's representation and participation within the union?

These research questions were addressed over a three-year period ending November 1995. Further details of the research approach and research sites can be found in Chapter 2 and in the Appendix. In brief, the research involved the extensive study of 15 representative bodies within UNISON. The decision-making bodies represented different aspects of UNISON's representative structure. Nine of these representative bodies derived from a mixed-sex constituency, the remainder deriving from a women-only constituency. Of the 15 decision-making bodies, eight operated at national level and seven operated at regional level. As discussed in Chapter 2, representative structures in UNISON are divided between those that relate to service-specific collective bargaining agenda and those that relate to union-wide non-collective bargaining agenda. Of the 15 institutions, four related to service-specific collective bargaining agenda and eleven related to union-wide non-collective bargaining agenda. Within each representative structure I collected material through observing meetings and educational activities, interviewing activists and paid officers and reading union documentation.

Presentation of the material

Chapter 2 provides the theoretical framework for the study of democratic change within UNISON. It starts by noting the difficulty of unravelling democracy and uses Sartori's (1965) work to differentiate between what is the reality of democracy (that is, descriptions of what exists) and what we think it should be (that is, prescriptions of we think should exist). Using Bachrach and Baratz's (1970) typology of power, the chapter illustrates how power over trade union members has been used for white, male members and identifies prescriptions to change the dominant practices of unionism to benefit women and other oppressed groups. The chapter ends with a research strategy for analysing the generation, and impact, of new sources of power for oppressed social groups within trade unions.

Chapters 3 to 9 are based on the case study research. Chapter 3 provides an examination of the development of UNISON and notes the extent to which UNISON's structure and rule-book commitments address the prescriptions noted in Chapter 2. Chapters 4 and 5 examine the implementation of proportionality in five mainstream committees. The chapters illustrate how these principles create a legitimate space for women representatives and enable democracy to be attained through the exclusion of men in proportion to their membership. However, whilst it is possible to change the rules of the game, the chapters identify a number of social processes which interact to determine the final outcome. Chapter 6 examines the implementation of fair representation and shows the implications of demands for class-based or job-based representation on the representation of black members.

Chapter 7 describes how women in two different geographical regions create a separate space in which to define their own interests. The two research sites provide very different interpretations, objectives and structures for women-only organisation in UNISON. One structure appears to challenge the male model of trade unionism and the other adapts it to the perceived needs of women. In the context of the wider union, the different structures raise questions about how the 'real' interests of women are best identified and served.

Chapters 8 and 9 focus on the content and practice of the union's mainstream decision-making arena and enable us to see how women's access to that arena can be translated into the discussion of the concerns of women. Chapter 8 illustrates that whilst women are gaining access to the national Local Government committee, not all women speak and few women speak of women's concerns. This contrasts with some of the observations seen in the regional structures examined in Chapter 9. Few women are silenced on this committee and more debates contain a gendered analysis. However, these discussions contrast with the issues raised in the women's structures. Each of these chapters identifies the institutional practices that prevent women talking and which inhibit women from talking for women. The chapters illustrate the contingent nature of the relationship between the election of individual women and the representation of women as a group.

Chapter 10 brings the themes of this study together in the context of earlier debates and explains why UNISON's structures are necessary but not sufficient. In relation to the latter argument, the chapter argues that women as a social group are still relatively powerless in relation to other groupings within the trade union. As a consequence there is too much reliance on individual women to push women's concerns. The chapter argues that unions should be organised around the representation of individuals and groups – a structure that UNISON has tentatively begun but needs to develop. That more could be achieved should not detract from the amount that has already been achieved. The chapter also emphasises that UNISON's structure contains some very necessary elements for gender democracy. Proportionality and fair representation have challenged norms of trade unionism and have altered political processes for women.   The chapter argues that these are necessary elements for all unions and other political organisations serious about gender democracy.

2 Making Sense of Democracy

The purpose of this chapter is to provide the reader with an analytical framework for understanding democratic processes within trade unions. It starts by following Sartori's (1965, 1987) example of differentiating between what is the reality of democracy (descriptions) and what we think it should be (prescriptions). Although democracy is constantly evolving, it always takes something of the former shape with it. That 'is' and 'ought' are never static has implications for the analysis of current reality. Should one begin one's analysis with the current 'ought' and 'is' or is an historical review necessary to provide an explanation of current descriptions and prescriptions?

Given that a comprehensive review would require the prescription and description of the role and identity of constituents, the role and identity of representatives and the role of the paid officers, I have forsaken this task. Instead, I focus on four main areas of debate. First, I describe Bachrach and Baratz (1970) analytical framework of power and decision making. Second, I apply this framework to indicate how democratic processes in trade unions have tended to favour white, male members. Third, I provide an overview of prescriptions for gender democracy and use Bachrach and Baratz's framework to explain how they could provide new sources of power for women and other oppressed social groups. The chapter ends with the research strategy that derives from these frameworks.

The analysis of democratic processes

Prescriptions and descriptions

Democracy is extraordinarily difficult to define and analyse. Sartori (1965, 1987) locates the problem of definition in the concept of democracy itself, noting that 'what democracy *is* cannot be separated from what democracy *should be*' (1987, p. 7, original emphasis). Sartori believes that this difficulty can be overcome by giving democracy a descriptive and prescriptive definition, a descriptive definition being that which describes what democracy 'is' in reality and a prescriptive definition being that which describes what an ideal democracy 'ought' to be. Sartori reiterates the dynamic nature of democracy by noting that the 'is' and the 'ought' of democracy are always interfering and colliding with each other. Indeed, he argues that 'democracy results from, and is shaped by, the interactions between its ideals and its reality, the pull of an *ought* and the resistance of an *is*' (ibid., p. 8, original emphasis). As this study will show, there is not one 'is' or 'ought', but using these terms does provide a useful framework for distinguishing the most relevant of the myriad of descriptions and prescriptions of trade union democracy. It also focuses attention on the omnipresent negotiation between prescriptions and descriptions. Integral to this negotiation are the 'rules of the game' (Bachrach and Baratz, 1970).

The rules of the game

Bachrach and Baratz argue that political systems develop a set of 'predominant values, beliefs, rituals, and institutional procedures' that operate consistently to the benefit of certain persons and groups at the expense of others. They call these values the 'rules of the game' and note that those who benefit from the rules are placed in a preferred position to defend and promote their vested interests through the 'mobilisation of bias' (1970, pp. 43–4). Bachrach and Baratz also provide a means for identifying how these preferred positions are shaped and maintained. They developed a typology of power and noted how groups maintained power through decisions and non-decisions.

Decisions

Bachrach and Baratz (1970) noted that decisions were those actions that required a choice be made from alternative options. They developed a typology of power and used it to show how 'A' could ensure that 'B' chose A's preferred option. They argued that the compliance of B was usually sought through the application of authority, influence and force and, to a lesser extent, power. Of relevance to this analysis is their definition of authority, influence and power. 'Authority' describes B's acceptance of A's option because it was reasonable and legitimate.

'Influence' describes B's acceptance of an argument through an obligation of respect for A. 'Power' describes B's acceptance of A's preferred option because A has threatened sanctions against B, which B wishes to avoid. Lukes (1974) noted the difficulty of defining a concept called 'power' in a typology of 'power' and suggested that this concept be renamed as 'coercion'. The subsequent text adopts Lukes' suggestion and uses the phrase 'coercive power' to denote those situations when A threatens sanctions against B, that B wishes to avoid. Given that representatives have few sanctions as such to use against each other, I have liberally interpreted 'sanctions' as being any form of action that would stop the normal course of representative decision making. Examples are threats of disruptions and demonstrations at committees, alliances with groups voting against the wishes of senior activists and paid officers and the use of veto powers.

Non-decisions

As noted above, A can use various forms of power to ensure that B complies with A's preferred options. Similarly, A could use these tactics to ensure that the rules of the game continue to favour A's own interests. However, Bachrach and Baratz (1970) argued that the primary method of ensuring that the rules of the game continued to be in A's interests is through a process of non-decision making. Bachrach and Baratz defined non-decisions as the 'suppression or thwarting of challenges to the values or interests of the decision-maker' (ibid., p. 44). They develop Schattschneider's earlier argument that 'some issues are organised into politics while others are organised out' (Schattschneider, 1960 in Lukes, 1974, p. 16) and note four forms of non-decision making that ensure that some issues are organised off the agenda.

First, force could be used to prevent demands for change entering the agenda. Second, issues could be kept off the agenda by the threat of sanctions (that is, coercion) against the initiator of potentially threatening demands. Third, norms, precedents or rules and procedures currently operating in the political system could be used to deny legitimacy to the initiator of new demands or deflect activity on their demands. Fourth, the rules of the game can be reinforced or reshaped to prevent issues getting on the agenda.

The 'rules of the game' in trade unions

Power over members

Trade unions enable members to exert a degree of control over their work. Fundamental to the power that unions use *for* members in their negotiations with employers, is the power that the union has *over* its members (Hyman, 1975, original emphasis). Thus a key issue in trade union democracy is ensuring that power over members is used for members. A number of studies have provided cause for such concerns. Amongst the first was the research that produced the concept of 'oligarchy' (Michels, 1915).

Drawing on research in the German socialist movement, Michels argued that leaders acquire, and retain, a relative influence within the political processes that is then used against the interests of the membership. He conceptualised this tendency for power to be used against members as the 'iron law of oligarchy' and attributed it to organisational and psychological factors. Leadership, Michels argues, brings importance, expertise, indispensability and a different lifestyle, which the leader seeks to protect by

> ...employing digressions, peri-phrases, and terminological subtleties, by means of which they surround the simplest matter with a maze of obscurity to which they alone have the clue. In this way, whether acting in good faith or in bad, they render it impossible for the masses, whose 'theoretical interpreters' they should be, to follow them, and to understand them, and they thus elude all possibility of technical control. They are masters of the situation. (Michels, 1915, p. 91)

In essence, paid officers were accused of maintaining their vested interests through the use of non-decision-making tactics. Michels' arguments prompted numerous studies within trade unions as many sought to confirm or refute these findings. Amongst these studies were those engaging with the representative dimension of democracy whereby union members elect representatives to act for them at a number of levels within the union. Writers such as Lipset et al. (1956), Edelstein (1967), and Martin (1968) argue that formal structures and regular elections, contested by groups and factions, provide new sources of power to members. These writers did not argue, however, with Michels' explanation for oligarchic tendencies. Hyman (1975) proffered another explanation for these tendencies.

Using a Marxist analysis of industrial relations, Hyman argued that broader structural determinants were necessary to explain this oligarchic tendency and attributed it to the relationship between capital and labour. His analysis led him to argue that officials were more likely to suppress irregular and disruptive activities than challenge managerial control. From this perspective, formal representative structures – such as branch committees, regional or national committees – were deemed inadequate to ensure that power over members was used for members by challenging employers. Instead, theorists such as Hyman argued that it was only through decisions made by and through shop stewards that power over members could be used for members. Writers such as Gouldner (1955), Hyman (1971a, 1971b), Lane (1974) and Fairbrother (1984) engaged with aspects of participatory democracy to argue that shop stewards provided unions with a countervailing 'iron law of democracy'. Their studies described how shop stewards were intimately involved in decision making, and the mobilisation of members on an informal basis at local level. Shop stewards were deemed to be in the best place to represent, and be representative of, their work colleagues. Work colleagues could displace shop stewards at any time and shop stewards could often operate in opposition to representatives elected to higher levels of union structures. Thus, new sources of power – particularly coercion, through the mobilisation of members and authority, through an immediate form of legitimisation by workplace colleagues – were generated to ensure that the rules of the game favoured members rather than paid officers and national representatives.

Although these debates have since moved on, the concepts retain their pertinence. Oligarchic tendencies haven't gone away, nor have representative structures or arguments for participatory democracy. Regarding the latter, prescriptions for the greater participation of trade union members are often viewed with suspicion. Government fears that 'militant' and 'unrepresentative' activists were taking members into politically motivated strike action prompted a raft of union legislation in the last twenty years. Successive legislation saw a narrowing of the definition of a legal dispute, union funds liable to seizure in illegal dispute activity and compulsory balloting prior to industrial action. If paid officers needed excuses to suppress irregular and disruptive activities, this legislation certainly provided them.

Power for all members

The aforementioned studies address Hyman's trade union democracy question of 'how can workers ensure that power over them is used in their collective interests?' They can be distinguished from those studies that address a different aspect of democracy – the identity of those making collective decisions about collective interests. These latter studies indicated that the majority of union representatives were white men, that women tended to participate at branch level only and that members' interests were defined by white men rather than women and black members (see Lawrence, 1994; Ledwith and Colgan, 1996 for reviews of these studies). If these findings are added to Hyman's (1989) acceptance that lay activists may be as far removed from the sentiments of their constituents as are the paid officials, the question of trade union democracy can be re-written as 'how can all workers ensure that power over them is used in the collective interests of everyone?'

This question has become particularly pertinent in the context of declining membership and the rise in the number of women workers and women members. It is in this context that newer prescriptions for union democracy have evolved. In his later work Hyman acknowledges that white, male, relatively skilled and higher paid workers dominate the hierarchy of activism within trade unions; he attributes this hierarchy to a set of social relations denoted as 'bureaucracy' (1989, pp. 181–2). He argues that this bureaucracy derives from the separation of representation from mobilisation, a hierarchy of control and activism, and the detachment of decision making from members' experiences. He calls for unions to build on the work of feminist critiques, community-based action groups and peace movements and identifies three major changes for unions:

- Unionism to be informed by workers' current experiences, aspirations, hopes, fears, grievances and enthusiasms.
- Existing disparate and fragmented struggles to be unified from the grassroots upwards.
- Trade union activities to be connected more directly with wider social movements and social struggles.

Hyman (1989) recognises that an essential issue is the co-ordination of activity so that divisive demands and strategies are avoided and special concern is shown for marginalised groups. In a later text, Hyman conceptualises these as issues of 'strategic leadership and democratic activism', noting that the challenge is to

> ...develop both stronger centralised structures and the mechanisms for more vigorous grassroots participation; which entails new kinds of articulation between the various levels of union organisation, representation and action. (1997, p. 532)

Of importance to future analysis is his argument that solidarity between different groupings within unions (for example, based on occupations or marginalisation) presupposes 'a process of internal education and argument of major extent and intensity' (Hyman, 1989, p. 185).

Fairbrother (1996) believes that Hyman's conceptualisation of 'bureacracy' lends itself to an overly pessimistic view of the future. Instead, Fairbrother argues that certain circumstances – such as state restructuring – support the emergence of new forms of participatory unionism. His research in public sector unions led him to identify three aspects of an emergent unionism. First, he identified the reintegration of representation and action such that representatives became 'part of the process of membership mobilisation as active participants'. Second, he saw more local members taking decisions that directly concerned their immediate work and employment relations. Third, he saw primacy given to the participation of members in decision making and policy formulation through membership meetings.

Although Fairbrother argues against Hyman's analysis, the processes prescribed and described in their respective works share similar characteristics, and both agree that this activity *must* come from the very lowest level of organisation. Analysed on a feature-by-feature basis, it is difficult to argue against these essential elements of democracy. Indeed, as will be seen later, features of inclusion, unification, social movements and active participation are essential features of the longest agenda of equal opportunities too. However, despite providing useful frameworks for 'representation and action', neither framework is sufficient of itself to displace the domination of unions by male, relatively skilled and higher paid workers. Although participation is a powerful force for change – and a key element of an equal opportunities agenda – the energy it generates needs to be focused into an institutional structure that addresses the power imbalance between different groups of members. In essence, participation is necessary, but not sufficient to change the dominant rules of the game in trade unions. Whilst concepts of bureaucracy may describe some elements of the political process, they do not adequately explain why it is men who continue to benefit from the rules of the game.

Power for men

A number of studies illustrate how men have used coercive power, authority, influence and force to exclude women from decision-making structures and suppress their concerns (see Beale (1982), Cockburn (1983), Colling and Dickens (1989), Cockburn (1991) and Cunnison and Stageman (1993)). The word 'representative' infers at least two duties of the representative: to represent the interests and views of the represented, and to share at least some of the characteristics of the represented (Holden, 1993, p. 59). Numerous surveys have shown that the latter duty is not being met. Women and black members are under-represented in union representative structures (Southern and Eastern Regional Council Women's Rights Committee, 2000). Case study research has provided much evidence of how the former duty remains unfulfilled too. In particular, these studies illustrate how non-decision making has been used to suppress women's challenges to men's vested interests in trade union power. A dominant form of this non-decision making has been the determination of the rules of the game in terms of male norms.

The construction of reality from men's experiences has been conceptualised as a 'male standard' (Briskin and McDermott, 1993b, p. 11) or 'male norms' (Bradley, 1999, p. 171). Briskin and McDermott identify two assumptions in the male standard. The first is that the 'experience of men is generic to both women and men'. The second is that men's reality establishes a 'norm' against which women are measured. Both assumptions have been used to exclude the concerns of women. The pervasive nature of these assumptions is illustrated by the work of Cyba and Papouschek (1996). These authors studied female workers in four sectors in Austria. Their research revealed that a large proportion of problems mentioned by women never went beyond the preliminary stages of 'confused discontent, dissatisfaction or assessment of the problem'. They noted that a number of 'objectively' disadvantageous workplace situations were frequently leading to no reaction from the women themselves. By reconstructing the manner in which problems were articulated, Cyba and Papouschek were able to conclude that the process was blocked from the outset by 'inner barriers'. They attributed these barriers to women's lack of social identity in the world of work and argued for new forms of workplace representation, which start from 'women's real life problems and experiences'. Whilst these arguments echo earlier prescriptions for grassroots participation and activism, they arguably still leave untouched the powerlessness of women in society.

Oppressed social groups

The bias towards the representation of white male interests is not confined to trade unions and political theorists of wider society can shed much light on the roots and remedies for oppression. Young (1990) provides us with a useful framework for identifying social groups and oppressed social groups. Young argues that social groups are not aggregates of individuals, but are defined through their social status, and the common history that social status produces. Young identifies five sites of oppression – exploitation, marginalisation, powerlessness, cultural imperialism and violence – which determine whether social groups are oppressed.

This is not to imply individuals, or social groups, are unified and homogeneous. Indeed, Young recognises that since individuals and social groups reflect the multitude of differentiation in wider society, they can be no other than heterogeneous with relations and affinities within and outside social groups being fluid and shifting. This said, these latter comments should not detract attention from Young's two main arguments. The first is that formal democratic processes often elevate the perspectives of materially privileged groups and silence those of oppressed groups. Second, oppressed social groups require institutional mechanisms to put them on an equal basis with materially privileged groups. The details of these institutional mechanisms are discussed below, but first, it is necessary to identify a particular democratic need distinct to the social group of women.

Women as an oppressed social group

Women are recognised as an oppressed social group because they are subject to 'gender-based exploitation, powerlessness, cultural imperialism and violence' (Young, 1990, p. 64). From Young's perspective, institutional mechanisms are required to empower the social group of women and as we shall see later, it is these prescriptions that underpin the longest agenda for equal opportunities in trade unions. In addition, a number of commentators would argue that empowering the social group of women requires a practical engagement between democratic processes and the private sphere of domestic life.

Theories of representative and participatory democracy assume that men and women have equal opportunities to engage in the democratic process of being a representative or participating in meetings. Whilst Young's prescriptions for oppressed social groups seek to equalise power between groups, they do not address the political consequences of women's greater role in the home. That is, they do not address the likelihood that women are less able to devote time to participating in the political process (Pateman, 1983). Pateman argues that if women are to be equal and full citizens, then radical changes are required at home, advocating that men and women need to share equally the responsibilities of domestic life.

A number of prescriptions seek to empower women. Each puts women as the heart of the analysis and starts from the premise that women have distinct democratic needs. They can be categorised within Cockburn's (1989) framework of the short and long agendas of equal opportunities. The shortest agenda contains prescriptions to counteract exclusion through domestic commitments and the longest agenda advocates representation by individuals of oppressed social groups *and* representation of oppressed social groups. These prescriptions are detailed below and Bachrach and Baratz's (1970) framework is used to identify the new sources of power they provide for women and other oppressed social groups.

Prescriptions for gender democracy

Prescriptions to address exclusion through domestic commitments

The shortest agenda of equal opportunities aims to minimise the bias against the representation and participation of those with domestic responsibilities. Initially targeted at women, who bear the greater burden of tasks within the home, the majority of trade unions acknowledge the need for family-friendly practices. Now targeted at both sexes, family-friendly practices include job-sharing for activists and paid officers, the provision of crèche facilities or childcare allowances for activists attending meetings. However, whilst family-friendly practices are a necessary condition to supporting the greater participation of women, they are insufficient in themselves to address the under-representation of women within unions.

Prescriptions for paid officers

As noted above, Hyman (1975) attributed oligarchic tendencies of paid officers to the structural determinants of capital and labour. Kelly and Heery (1994) argue for accepting a more voluntarist account of the activities of the paid union official. Their analysis of trade union democracy revealed the different orientations and values that paid union officers bring to their work enabling them to deploy a range of choices at their own discretion. In particular, they found that the new generation of women officers was playing a more radical role in organising and promoting women's interests in the labour movement (see also Heery and Kelly, 1988a, 1988b, 1989). Such descriptions of activity by women paid officers have led to prescriptions for the removal of restrictive recruitment practices (that work against under-represented groups) and the active employment of more women paid officers. Drawing on extensive research in a number of unions, Cunnison and Stageman (1993) present an argument for feminising the job of the paid officer – through the employment of more women and changing the nature of the job. Unions are increasing the number of women paid officers, but as indicated by Cockburn (1993), this does meet with male resistance. Heery and Kelly's survey of paid women officers indicates the difficulty of the working environment for women. Over half of their sample reported that they were 'sometimes' subject to sexual discrimination at work from colleagues and members, and about a fifth of the women reported that they were 'sometimes' subject to sexual harassment (1988b, p. 94). This prompted another prescription from Heery and Kelly (1989) – that unions should discourage sexist behaviour.

Kelly and Heery's (1994) analysis of trade union democracy also led them to argue that the decentralisation of power to workplaces in previous decades was acting against the interests of members in marginalised groups, particularly women, in the very different conditions of the 1980s and 1990s. Kelly and Heery argue that the absence of full employment, corporate profitability, government support for trade unionism and a permissive legal climate, exposes the weakness of workplace bargaining and the preoccupation of local paid officers and stewards with organised workers in organised workplaces. One prescription for change was the centralisation of power in order to conserve, mobilise and target resources on priority issues such as membership recruitment and campaigns over women's rights.

Prescriptions for representative structures

A number of writers argue that reserving seats for women is a necessary condition for guaranteeing representation by women in parity with men (Trebilcock, 1991; Nightingale, 1991). Cockburn (1996) denotes such strategies as those that identify women as 'individuals in a sex-category'. Women are distinguished from others by their biological sex and seats can be reserved for them in specific, absolute numbers (often referred to as 'quotas') or in proportion to the number of women in the constituency (often referred to as 'proportionality'). Multi-representative constituencies aid this process (Cockburn, 1996). Increasingly, arguments are being made for the reservation of seats for individuals from other oppressed social groups, such black members, disabled members, gay and lesbian members and young members. A recent survey of 27 unions, representing 80 per cent of the TUC affiliated membership indicates that seven of the 27 unions use reserved seats for women and three reserve seats for black members (Southern and Eastern Regional TUC Women's Rights Committee, 2000).

Enabling members of oppressed social groups to take seats on representative structures ensures that some of the representatives will share some of the characteristics of the represented. If the seat taken by the individual member of the oppressed social group would otherwise have been taken by an individual from an over-represented privileged group, then this reallocation of seats provides a form of 'basic justice' (Phillips, 1991). It also provides those individuals with a new source of authority in decision making. For example, women may be more able to persuade other decision-makers to take up their preferred options, if they themselves are part of the decision-making process. However, the election of individual members of oppressed social groups does not guarantee that they will pursue the concerns of the oppressed social group. Since one of the duties of the representative is to represent the interests and views of the represented, if a woman, for example, is elected from a mixed-sex constituency, then she has no obligation to pursue the concerns of women (Cockburn, 1996).

Prescriptions for women-only structures

Cunnison and Stageman argue that a strategy that only seeks to increase the number of women in representative positions 'still leaves the pervasive hold of male culture, the underpinning of formal and informal male power'. Their prescription for improving women's representation is one that 'guarantees women space to develop their collective ideas and a platform from which to make themselves heard' (1993, pp. 167–8). A number of unions have accepted this principle and over time this support has evolved from resourcing women-only advisory groups to women's self-organisation (see Briskin, 1999).

Studies by Cobble (1990), Cockburn (1991), Cunnison and Stageman (1993) and Briskin and McDermott (1993a) illustrate how self-organisation represents a significant lengthening of the equal opportunities agenda. These studies indicate the ability of women-only groups to challenge male norms underpinning present forms of trade unionism. In essence, they provide oppressed social groups, rather than individuals, with new sources of authority and influence. Studies have also revealed that self-organised groups have a tendency to forge alliances and coalitions outside the union, with wider social movements and social struggles (Briskin and McDermott, 1993a; Cunnison and Stageman, 1993). Similar studies illustrate the transformational power of self-organisation for other marginalised groups such as black members (Virdie and Grint, 1994), and gay and lesbian members (Colgan, 2000).

The potential for self-organised groups to ensure that decision making engages with workers' experiences is demonstrated most graphically in Cunnison and Stageman's study of women's organisation in NUPE Northern Ireland. In their study, they note that during wage claims:

> NUPE Northern Ireland held branch meetings where members examined their wage slips to see the precise effects the current claim would have on them personally. In one such exercise, part-timers found that virtually every woman in the room who was working less than 8–20 hours had in fact lost pay every time she had had a pay rise. This had come about either through a cut in hours or through moving into a poverty trap. (1993, p. 227)

A number of unions have recognised the importance of encouraging women's participation through women-only groups. In a recent survey, 13 of 27 UK unions provided some form of women-only structures (Southern and Eastern Regional TUC Women's Rights Committee, 2000). However, it is important to distinguish the nature of that support.

Briskin's (1993, 1999) work indicates that women's voices and perspectives are heard when unions underpin self-organised groups with resources, decision-making powers, protective mandates, direct input into organisational decision making, links to the collective bargaining process and union-wide communication potential. This is a comprehensive list and straddles what Briskin calls an 'autonomy – integration paradigm'. On the one hand, self-organised groups legitimise themselves through their autonomy from the mainstream structures (underpinned by resources, decision-making powers and protective mandates) and on the other, they require a decision-making role within mainstream structures (integration).

A framework developed by Pateman (1970) can be used to determine the extent to which self-organised groups are genuinely involved in decision making. Pateman made a distinction between partial participation, pseudo-participation, and full participation. Partial participation describes those situations where participants have the ability to influence decisions, but the final decision will rest elsewhere. Pseudo-participation refers to situations where participants are asked to accept decisions that have already been made. Full participation happens when each member of the decision-making body has equal power to determine the outcome of the decisions. Without direct input into organisational decisions and links to the collective bargaining process, self-organised groups have very little authority and influence in mainstream structures.

At best, they would have partial participation or, at worst, pseudo-participation. If unions provide these links – thereby enabling full participation – then the agenda for equal opportunities is arguably longer than that inferred by prescriptions for women-only structures. As such, it arguably starts from another point – that of equalising power between oppressed social groups and privileged groups.

Prescriptions for group representation

Advocating strong links between mainstream committees and women's groups is not a new prescription (Trebilcock, 1991) but it is starting to take a different form. Cockburn (1996) develops the work of Young (1990) and argues that trade unions should provide for the representation of women as an oppressed social group. This requires a qualitatively different structure to that which merely supports women-only groups. As noted above, Young believes it is possible to counteract the bias towards privileged groups. She advocates the provision of 'mechanisms for the effective recognition and representation of the distinct voices and perspectives of those of its constituent groups that are oppressed or disadvantaged'. More specifically, Young argues for the provision of

> ...(1) self-organization of group members so that they achieve collective empowerment and a reflective understanding of their collective experience and interests in the context of the society; (2) group analysis and group generation of policy proposals in institutionalized contexts where decisionmakers are obliged to show that their deliberations have taken group perspectives into consideration; and (3) group veto power regarding specific policies that affect a group directly, such as reproductive rights policy for women, or land use policy for Indian reservations. (1990, p. 184)

From Young's perspective, self-organisation is part of the larger process of group representation. The importance of self-organisation lies in the space it provides for oppressed groups to determine their own interests away from the influence of the privileged group. The importance of the latter two mechanisms lies in the rights they provide to representation. By providing for the group analysis and generation of proposals which decision makers are obliged to take into account, these prescriptions provide oppressed social groups with a constant source of authority and influence on mainstream structures. This authority and influence is arguably stronger than that obtainable by self-organised groups which, as indicated by Briskin (1999), continually need to strike a strategic balance between autonomy and integration. By providing groups with veto power on matters that concern them, oppressed social groups are gaining the ability to win arguments through the use of coercive power, that is, the threat of sanctions. Although the use of Lukes' term 'coercion' infers that this form of power is undesirable, it arguably provides oppressed social groups with more negotiating capacity than can be obtained through sources of power (such as authority and influence) obtained through being an individual representative.

This model of representation is very different from rights of representation that are traditionally derived from the election of individuals to representative positions. This means that representation of social groups is not dependent on the election of individuals who are also members of oppressed social groups or are sympathetic to their aims. Nor does the concept rely entirely on structures of representative democracy. Instead, Young's (1990) framework provides a means by which participatory democracy feeds into representative democracy and group representation is given legitimacy alongside individual representation.

Organising unions around group representation is qualitatively different because it challenges some of the basic principles of democracy. In particular, it challenges the idea that decisions are made by individual representatives elected by the whole people. Instead, group representation provides self-organised groups with an explicit role in making decisions that is derived from institutional rules rather than negotiated over time. Moreover, groups gain access to decision making because of their societal status not through their election by the whole people. In essence, it is problematic to equate the representative who has gained legitimacy through open election with the representative who has gained legitimacy through their membership of a social group (Phillips, 1991, 1993, 1999). Phillips identifies two arguments against group representation.

The first argument relates to the specific issue of group representation of women. Phillips notes that present forms of representative democracy are based on political rather than social groups. She argues that this ensures that there are few mechanisms for enabling women's voices to be heard or women's perspectives to be agreed. In the absence of effective mechanisms for interest aggregation amongst women, Phillips concludes that the representation of women, as a group, rests 'too exclusively on trust' (1991 p. 91).

The second argument relates to the nature of group representation. Phillips' makes an additional observation about the difference between interest groups and social groups (which she calls 'identity groups'). Whilst noting that social groups, or identity groups, are defined by a common experience of exclusion, Phillips argues that these identities are 'often secured in direct opposition to some "other"' (1993, p. 17). This leads her to argue that 'the intensity of identity politics is less amenable to a politics of accommodation or compromise, and is far more likely to encourage fragmentation or mutual hostility.' This approach is contrasted with that of interest-group pluralism which, she argues, lends itself to groups organising around interests and 'more happily' reaching accommodation with alternative concerns. This is not a description that Young (1990) would recognise, having argued that group representation provides an antidote to 'self deceiving self-interest masked as impartial or general interest'.

A more positive view of interest aggregation amongst women can be seen in trade union studies by Cockburn (1991), Cunnison and Stageman (1993), Briskin and McDermott (1993a) and Briskin (1999). Given that Phillips' work concerns societal politics, it is tempting to conclude that trade unions are more able to organise suitable structures for social groups which, in turn, are more likely to forge alliances across groups. In her study of women's organisation in NUPE Northern Ireland, Cockburn noted that women forged alliances with men who might 'otherwise feel angered, alienated or rejected by the union'. Women in the study argued that it was in men's interests that women's interests were protected because increasing the value of someone else 'increases the value they have themselves' (1991, p. 133). This confirms the conclusion reached by Leidner in her study of the National Women's Studies Association in the US, that 'full satisfaction [of minority interests] would apparently require that those in the majority wholly identify the interests of the minorities as their own' (1991, p. 228). From such descriptions, come prescriptions for the involvement of working-class women, the development of alliances with supportive men (Cockburn, 1991, p. 234) and the practice of democracy within women-only groups, thus 'ensuring the inclusion of particularly disadvantaged groups of women' (Cockburn, 1996, p. 4).

*Prescriptions for representation by individuals of oppressed social groups **and** representation of oppressed social groups*

At the time of writing, these prescriptions represent the longest equal opportunities agenda in trade unions. They build on Cockburn's (1996) work on gender democracy. Cockburn conceptualises gender democracy in terms of women's access and engagement in policy-making forum and provision for women's particular concerns to be adequately voiced. For Cockburn, gender democracy can be achieved through structures that provide for representation by women as individuals *and* the representation of women as a social group. The first strategy is a necessary condition for guaranteeing individual women a full role in policy formulation. The second strategy is a necessary condition for counteracting the power of materially privileged groups and ensuring that women's concerns are not silenced or denigrated by those groups. This does not mean that women will be over-represented. Any woman elected to represent a women-only group on a mainstream committee would be expressly elected to represent the concerns of women as a social group (Cockburn, 1996). As Cockburn indicates, this is different to women elected to the same committee from mixed-sex constituencies who may well bring a woman's perspective to the committee but are not obliged to speak for women as a group. In essence, these prescriptions provide new sources of authority and influence to individual women and new sources of authority, influence and coercive power to women as a social group.

When Cockburn made these arguments, she was specifically focusing on gender democracy, but the study of UNISON suggests that prescriptions already exist for pulling trade union democracy towards a more inclusive model (see also Colgan, 2000). It is argued that women have distinct democratic needs that derive from the patriarchal social order determined at the beginning of new civil society (see Pateman, 1988). That other citizens have distinct democratic needs that derive from sites of oppression such as institutional racism and homophobia also needs to be acknowledged in the representative structures of unions.

Implications for research in UNISON

UNISON – a new union

This chapter has identified key issues in trade union democracy and made two distinctions for future analysis. First, a distinction has been made between prescriptions that seek women's empowerment through universal participatory structures and those that seek it through specific structures for women. Of the latter strategies, a distinction has been made between self-organisation and group representation. In each case, as we shall see in Chapter 3, UNISON's structure appears to follow the more radical strategy. First, the rule book provides specific structures for women's representation. Second, the rule book provides for some form of group representation. Together, these commitments generate new sources of authority and influence for individual women and new sources of authority, influence and coercive power for women as a social group.

This outcome is the result of considerable activity in the merger negotiations. Fryer (2000) refers to the desire that UNISON would be a recognisably 'new' union and would not be merely the sum of its former partner unions. A key element of this 'newness' was the desire for new structures and organisation, which built fair representation into the core of its arrangements. According to the final report of the former partner unions to their members (COHSE, NALGO, NUPE, 1992), equal opportunities and fair representation were of paramount importance to the new union.

The study of UNISON in its first three years of development provides a rich illustration of the different social processes that shape democracy and the implications of these processes for men and women members. Bachrach and Baratz (1970, pp. 50–51) argue that their suggested approach to the analysis of power addresses questions of how new sources of coercive power, authority and influence are generated and how they alter the political process and lessen inequality between groups and individuals. The following sections indicate how their framework has been applied to this study of UNISON.

The generation of new sources of power

As indicated above, UNISON is distinctive in the manner in which it has engaged with each of the aforementioned prescriptions for gender democracy. The aim of these prescriptions is to provide individual women, and women as a social group, with the ability to influence decision making to the same extent as men. They also seek to change the dominant values within trade unions such that men are less able to determine the rules of the game and defend their vested interests in positions of power. Understanding how these new sources of power for women have been generated and shaped enables us to address wider questions of gender democracy and trade union democracy. In particular this framework enables us to reflect on the interaction of different strategies, understand how the rules of the game can be changed and identify forms of resistance and accommodation. Such questions were addressed through the detailed study of rule-book commitments to proportionality, fair representation, and self-organisation. Since this study started after the merger date of July 1993, the research focuses on how these rule-book commitments were introduced and shaped in each of the research sites.

As noted in Chapter 1 and the Appendix, these research sites were chosen to provide a cross-section of the national and regional representative structures in the union. Although the principles of proportionality and fair representation applied from the creation of the union, in effect they were only enacted through the creation of substantive UNISON committees (as opposed to interim committees consisting of members elected from the former partner unions). Substantive UNISON regional and national committees were created well in advance of UNISON branches which were still in the process of merging during the period of this study and in many cases remained ostensibly COHSE, NALGO and NUPE branches. Branches were not therefore the focus of analysis.

I examined the constitution and election processes of six mainstream representative structures at national level: the National Delegate Conference (NDC), the National Executive Council (NEC), the Local Government Service Group (LGSG) Executive and Conference and the Health Care Service Group (HCSG) Executive and Conference. At regional level, I examined the constitution and election processes of a Regional Council and Regional Committee in two regions. The regions are identified as Region 1 and 2 in the text – which bears no relationship to their geographical numbering within UNISON. The range and number of these committees enabled me to compare the development of the same principle across all committees, between regions, between national and regional levels, between service group committees and between service and non-service group committees.

I was given generous access to all of these structures (with the exception of the NEC). Given that UNISON was in its early stages of development during my study, I was able to observe the development of these new sources of power in a range of representative structures. This detailed observation of decision making was supplemented with an examination of written constitutions and formal interviews, and informal discussions, with committee members and paid officers associated with each committee. I performed a similar task in relation to the constitution and election processes of six women-only structures. These were the National Women's Committee; the National Women's Conference; and Regional Committees and Conferences in Regions 1 and 2. My observation of all of these committees is discussed below.

The impact of UNISON's strategies on political processes

In addition to noting how UNISON's strategies were evolving, this study endeavoured to note the impact of these strategies on political processes. Bachrach and Baratz (1970) suggest that a detailed study of the decision-making process yields valuable clues about the prevailing rules of the game and which groups are being disadvantaged as a result of those rules. They also suggest that particular attention should be paid to those issues that involve a genuine challenge to the resources of power of those currently dominating the process of decision making. I attended 64 union meetings over the period of this study – details of which are in the Appendix. Two mainstream structures and three women-only structures were regularly attended over the period of a year.

I took detailed notes at these meetings as a means of understanding how individuals and groups interacted to create, maintain and change dominant values and institutional practices. I was interested in the attendance, behaviour and priorities of everyone in the meeting – men and women, paid officers and members. I was also interested in the content of the meetings and took a keen interest in the agenda and the issues that were discussed. Of the considerable material collected, I focused my attention on two main issues: implementation of the rule book commitments to gender democracy; and issues of concern to women. A further distinction was made between observable decision-making processes and non-decision-making processes.

The one-dimensional view of power is the name that Lukes (1974) gives to the study of the observable behaviour of decision-makers. Although criticised for its restrictive view of power, the detailed study of decision making does provide valuable information about which participants initiate policy that is eventually adopted, who suggests alternative policies that are defeated and who votes for which option. So, for example, I noted how individuals and particular groupings responded to the implementation of the rule-book commitments. Were any patterns discernable, say, in the behaviour of women, or paid officers? Were these patterns replicated across time, or across committees?

Bachrach and Baratz (1970) provide a framework for understanding how the compliance of participants can be sought through the application of authority, influence, force and coercive power, but these definitions are relatively imprecise when one wishes to operationalise them. The detailed study of shop stewards conducted by Batstone et al. (1977) was concerned to understand how members persuaded others to follow them, but declined to make any distinction between power and authority, and power and influence. Instead, the authors admitted to using the term power very broadly. I felt it necessary however, to distinguish between different forms of power (see also Bradley (1999) who conceptualises gendered power in the workplace and identifies nine dimensions of power related to the use of different resources).

My reading of Young's (1990) work is that the equalisation of power between privileged and oppressed social groups is distinct from the equalisation of power sought through an increase in representation by individuals of oppressed social groups. If these strategies provide different forms of power to oppressed social groups, then there is a need to make this distinction in case study analysis. I have therefore used Bachrach and Baratz's four terms to bring some distinction to the analysis of power and decision-making in UNISON. Authority has been used to describe the power articulated by majority decision-makers. Influence has been used to describe power that is articulated by those in positions of influence, such as paid officers or lay chairpersons. Coercive power has been used to describe power that is articulated through the threat of sanctions, such as the withdrawal of votes for particular issues or unconstitutional activity. The one-dimensional view of power described above required a focus on which individuals and groups were winning the arguments and, by implication, shaping democracy in UNISON. However, as Lukes indicates, a methodology that only focuses on concrete decisions and observable behaviour hides the articulation of other forms of power.

The two-dimensional view of power is the name that Lukes gave to the study of non-decision-making. As noted earlier, Bachrach and Baratz (1970) believe that non-decision-making is a primary method of exerting power. This view of power prompted me to pay particular attention to members who did not speak and issues that were not discussed. This was by way of determining the extent to which some groups might be mobilising bias in their favour and keeping certain items off the agenda. Bachrach and Baratz address the difficult question of how an outside observer can determine whether the rules of the game are being supported by non-decisions. They suggest that the investigator records any grievances that are expressed within or outside of the political system and endeavours to determine why and by what means these grievances have been denied an airing. The grievances to which I paid particular attention related to the implementation of the three rule-book commitments to gender democracy and issues of concern to women. As will be seen later, some grievances were expressed within formal structures and others were gleaned from personal interviews. The study of proportionality and fair representation across a number of committees also provided a useful indicator of where some participants might be organising some issues off the agenda. In this respect it was useful to use the concepts of 'silence' and 'din' to describe the domination and subordination operating in certain decision-making arenas (Harlow et al., 1995).

It was also my intention to analyse the research material using the three-dimensional view of power developed by Lukes. Having argued that the two-dimensional view of power provided an inadequate framework of analysis, Lukes identified another form of power. This was an unseen power that provided groups with the means of controlling the terms of debates such that those disfavoured by the decision-making processes were not even aware that they should have grievances – that is, their 'real' interests were suppressed. At first sight, this appeared to be a useful means of explaining the existence of male standards and male norms. It also provides a means of explaining why women were not reacting to 'objectively' disadvantageous workplace situation in the study of Cyba and Papouschek's (1996). In the end, however, this framework of analysis was not used. First, it was difficult to operationalise. If the suppression of real interests is discovered, this places the researcher in the uncomfortable position of being more 'knowing' than those supposedly being disfavoured. If real interests are not discovered, then how does the researcher know whether this reflects the suppression of their own real interests? A second reason for not pursuing this form of analysis relates to the considerable amount of material that could be analysed from the two-dimensional view of power. The triangulation of material from comparative committees, observations of committee meetings and interview data suggested a degree of non-decision making that required further exploration.

These observations have provided a rich source of material for this study. I have reproduced a number of these observations in this text, together with relevant extracts of speeches and interviews because they effectively illuminate a number of the social processes within UNISON. When frequent reference is made to particular members, I have used names but in each case this is not the person's real name. I supplemented these observations with formal interviews and informal discussions with committee members and paid officers and documentary evidence.

3 UNISON in the Making

A distinction was made in the last chapter between prescriptions for trade union democracy and those for gender democracy. In particular, I argued that calls for 'representation and action' were necessary but not sufficient to displace male domination of unions. Instead, I argued that prescriptions that put the empowerment of oppressed social groups at the heart of their analysis – in this case, women – were needed to guarantee the equal representation of women as individuals and women as a social group. As noted earlier, UNISON's structures and rule book do match some of these prescriptions.

It was the express intention of UNISON to empower its members, both as employees and as citizens, through a redefinition of its purpose and its creation of a member-led union. In particular, the adoption of three key principles – proportionality for women, fair representation at all levels and self-organisation for four disadvantaged groups (women, black, lesbian and gay, and disabled members) – was intended to have a significant impact on the nature of women's involvement in the union. This chapter analyses the manner in which new sources of power were generated for women and other oppressed social groups. It draws on proposals for the new union (COHSE, NALGO, NUPE, 1990, 1991, 1992) written accounts of the merger process, policy outcomes in the form of the UNISON rule book (UNISON, 1993, 1994a, 1997a), the 'Code of Good Branch Practice' (UNISON, 1994b) and guidelines on proportionality (1994c), fair representation (1997b) and self-organisation (1998a). Material was also collected through interviews with senior activists and paid officers involved in the merger. This chapter deals with three main issues.

First, it illustrates the extent to which traditional trade union issues dominated merger discussions. Second, it analyses the concepts of proportionality, fair representation and self-organisation and argues that they indicate a pursuit of gender democracy, but fall short of putting oppressed social groups at the heart of the constitution. Third, it indicates that at vesting day, much remained unresolved within UNISON, ensuring that many issues of democracy would be negotiated at a later date. The chapter concludes that UNISON has come close to reshaping certain aspects of democracy but that the final structure has been heavily influenced by arguments about which – and how – groups can continue to mobilise bias in their favour.

Organisational context

Although it was the express intention of the new union to empower members, there was much discussion about the best way of achieving this. When discussing the difficulty of defining democracy, Sartori noted that 'what democracy *is* cannot be separated from what democracy *should be*' (1987, p. 7, original emphasis). Analysis of the merger discussions (see Terry, 1996; Fryer, 2000) illustrates that when it comes to developing new constitutions, it is appropriate to turn Sartori's sentence around to read 'what democracy *should be* cannot be separated from what democracy *is*.' That is, the prescriptions put forward in the merger negotiations often reflected what already existed in the union making the suggestions. Two sets of differences are of particular interest to this study – those relating to the lay activist – paid officer relationship and those relating to equal opportunities strategies.

Lay activist – paid officer relationship

As noted in Chapter 2, the role of the paid officer is a contested issue with each union adopting its own practices for the relationship between paid officers and members. In NALGO, paid officers had no right to attend NALGO branches. In addition, NALGO branches retained the collected subscriptions of their membership. This enabled them to support industrial, political and educational activity at a local level – sometimes action that was independent of, and contrary to, national policy. The role of paid officers in NALGO is often contrasted with the role of paid officers in COHSE and NUPE. There were no rules in either union barring the involvement of paid officers at branch level and paid officers held key regional posts.

However, the presence or absence of these rules did not necessarily lead to dramatically different ways of working. An anthropologist's report conducted prior to the merger (Ouroussoff, 1993) argues that the description of NALGO being member-led and COHSE and NUPE being officer-led hid more than it revealed. Contrary to expectations, some

NALGO branches did rely on full-time officers and some COHSE and NUPE branches hardly saw a paid officer. More seriously, these myths and concerns dictated the terms of the merger negotiations and 'had fateful implications for elements and stages of the negotiations to establish a new union' (Fryer, 2000, pp. 39–40). The concern to retain or contain membership independence reflected broader concerns about the political position of the union.

NALGO was not affiliated to the Labour Party and often forged its own political perspective to the left of Labour Party trade union affiliates (Kelly, 1998). This contrasted with NUPE's relationship with the Labour Party. Although NUPE had been a militant opponent of Labour Government pay policies in the 1970s, the union was an affiliated member of the Labour Party and was working closely to see it re-elected. Indeed, the Deputy General Secretary of NUPE was a leading advocate of Labour Party change and modernisation, becoming Labour Party General Secretary in 1993/4 (Fryer, 2000). A more detailed discussion of this issue of political affiliation can be found in Jones (2000).

Equal opportunities strategies

At the time of merger, a distinctive feature of NUPE's equal opportunities was the reservation of seats for women on the national executive and regional committees. A recent review of equal opportunities policies in COHSE had recommended that one seat per region be allocated on their national executive for women candidates. Thus, both unions were prepared to use quotas (although not proportionality) to facilitate women's access to representative structures. This approach can be compared with the absence of such strategies in NALGO. Although it had originally reserved a seat for women on its national executive in 1924, this had been discontinued.

The distinctive feature of NALGO's equal opportunities structures was self-organisation for black members, members with disabilities and lesbian and gay members, which had evolved at branch, regional and national level over the previous decade. Although self-organised groups were not formally integrated into the main union structure they were consulted on some issues (see Kealey, 1990). However, as illustrated by Virdie and Grint (1994), self-organisation was a contested issue within NALGO and did not operate in all regions. COHSE's structures included a national Women's Committee and equal opportunities structures at regional and national level. NALGO's structures included a National

Women's Committee and National Women's Conference and equal opportunities committees at regions and branches. NUPE's structures included women's advisory committees at national and regional level.

Empowering members

That each former partner union was keen to retain at least some of its former identity and structure is not unique to UNISON.   What is important to note is that these arguments concerned the relationship between gender-neutral members and gender-neutral paid officers. Terry (1996) provides a useful insight into the negotiations that created the governing structures of UNISON. In particular, his account exposes the extent to which concerns about the possible exclusion of members were related to lay members in general, rather than women and oppressed groups in particular. He describes how NALGO's 'greatest concerns' set the negotiating agenda to which COHSE and NUPE responded, and discusses the ideological and practical differences between NUPE and COHSE on the one side and NALGO on the other.

The implications of this approach are discussed in the following sections. The first section reviews the dominant democracy arguments, indicating the structures that arose from these debates and noting unresolved issues. The second section reviews rule-book commitments to proportionality, fair representation and self-organisation. In particular, it argues that oppressed social groups could have been given more power if the union had been structured around their needs, rather than the needs of existing privileged groups.

In the interests of members: Part I

Tensions between grassroots strategies and joint determination

Terry's (1996) work and that of Fryer (2000) illustrate the competing prescriptions for empowering members. NALGO's chief concern was to develop a structure that would facilitate members through grassroots strategies. This structure required branch autonomy and lay control at all levels of the union. These prescriptions reflected the desire to maintain the strength of NALGO branches and perceptions of excessive officer involvement in COHSE and NUPE branches.

Fryer describes the competing model of democracy put forward by NUPE representatives, and supported by COHSE. They argued for breaking with the 'conventional preoccupation with producer interests and "bureaucratic" methods'. NUPE negotiators wanted to establish a new relationship between paid officers and members, based on 'partnership', and to 'shift influence from the minority of 'activists' to the 'membership at large'. Emphasis was on matters of 'organisational change, change management and the *joint* determination of future strategy by senior paid officers and national lay representatives'(Fryer, 2000, p. 33, original emphasis).

Chapter 2 made reference to Kelly and Heery's (1994) argument that decentralisation of power in trade unions was acting against the interests of marginalised groups such as women. Terry's (1996) review of the merger process, however, does not suggest that the potential for adverse links between autonomy and equal opportunities was an issue. For example, a gendered analysis might have raised the downside of branch autonomy for women. As more funds are retained at branch level, the less membership activities are funded from the centre. This in turn provides branch secretaries with considerable power and discretion over the distribution of funds, which could be to the detriment of funding oppressed social groups.

Thus, from both sides, the main debate concerned how control was to be maintained for gender-neutral members – not how members of oppressed social groups could be empowered. More detail of the debates can be found in Terry (1996) and Fryer (2000). These reveal that, despite considerable negotiation between the parties, issues of branch autonomy and lay control remained unresolved at the creation of the union (Fryer, 2000). As the report of the three unions' National Executives to the 1991 Annual Conferences indicates, union democracy within the new union appears to straddle prescriptions for lay autonomy and partnership. The approach of the new union emphasised:

> ...union democracy; membership involvement; lay representation and control at all levels; regional co-ordination; the acceptance of a strong and authoritative centre at the heart of the New Union; partnership between lay and employed officials at all levels; and the development of autonomous, well-resourced and clearly identified Service Groups. (COHSE, NALGO, NUPE, 1991, p. 45)

Whilst a major part of the merger discussions related to competing models of the member – officer relationship, attempts were also made to maintain the strength of former partner unions. This is seen most clearly in the merger debates concerning the organisational structure of UNISON.

Maintaining former partner unions

Fryer (2000) indicates that COHSE negotiators were keen to ensure that the larger numbers of NALGO and NUPE members did not numerically overwhelm former COHSE members and officers. The establishment of 'service groups' was seen as the one means that COHSE had of ensuring the creation of a section specifically for members employed in the health sector. Fryer credits the establishment of service groups within the new union to the single-mindedness of COHSE representatives who related 'virtually every aspect of the proposed new union's structure to their preferred organisation on the basis of service groups'.

According to its rule book, UNISON pursues two main areas of interests (UNISON, 1993). Under the heading of 'service groups', UNISON pursues matters affecting the pay and working conditions of employees. Under the heading of 'work and community', UNISON pursues matters 'affecting members (and their families) where it acts as a pressure group in the workplace and in society at large'. For the remainder of this book, the term 'service group structure' will be used to denote the mainstream committees that relate to the negotiation of pay and working conditions. The term 'non-service group structure' will be used to denote those mainstream committees that have no relationship to the negotiation of pay and working conditions.

Service group structures

Every member belongs to a branch that is based on the constituency of the employer. At its creation, each branch belonged to one of seven service groups: electricity, gas, health care, higher education, local government, transport and water. Electricity and gas have since merged to form an 'energy service group'. Although a number of working conditions may be negotiated at the local level, the terms and conditions of many members are still negotiated through their service group at a national level. National policy for service groups is agreed at service group conferences. National service group executives have responsibility for policy, the budget and the direction of the group's operations. A service group committee at regional level acts as an intermediary between branches and national structures. Although COHSE had won this argument, this was not the end of the negotiations.

Whilst the majority of seats on the Local Government and Health Care SGEs are obtained through direct election, a number of seats (six and eight respectively) are filled through the indirect election of representatives from Sector Committees. In addition to electing representatives to the SGE, the Sector Committees provide an opportunity for indirectly elected representatives to play a major part in the service group's decision making. The development of Sector Committees has its roots in the manner in which SGE members were elected in former partner unions. Some members believe that indirect elections allow for choice based on ability. A former NALGO member noted that the union

> ...could not afford to have airheads negotiating with employers. Those sent indirect from the region were known to have ability; to be reasonably articulate; have experience; and a few years at regional level – they would have served their time.

Another former NALGO member noted that direct elections 'knocked off experienced activists', as the voters did not necessarily know about union activity and activists. Both members noted, however, that the indirect system tended to filter out all groups which face disadvantage within society and, in particular, produce a disproportionate number of men.

The difference in opinion between direct and indirect elections for the SGEs was reconciled through the establishment of Sector Group Committees. The Local Government framework ensures that 'indirectly elected' members of Sector Committees are involved in collective bargaining, and 'directly elected' members of the SGEs are not directly involved in negotiations. This framework reflects the philosophy on directly elected seats of former NALGO members, who held the majority of seats on the Interim SGE. This contrasts with the responsibilities of the SGE in the Health Care Service Group, which ensures that although the group has sector groups, it is the directly elected SGE that is the highest authority within the group. This reflects the philosophy of former COHSE members who were directly elected and held the majority of seats on the interim SGE.

Non-service group structures

Each branch also operates within the non-service group structure. Members, shop stewards and branches can pursue non-service group issues at a local, regional and national level. Each branch belongs to one of 13 geographical regions. Within each region, Regional Council and Regional Committee provide opportunities for members from across all service groups to meet together and pursue wider concerns. Members also pursue non-service group issues at the annual National Delegate Conference that is the supreme decision-making body of the union. The National Executive Council (NEC) which, again, deals with non-service group issues, takes general management and control of the union between National Delegate Conferences (NDCs). Individual members can be elected to Regional Committee, Regional Council, the NEC and the NDC.

The distinction between service and non-service group structures has important implications for the location of power in UNISON. Fryer (2000) notes that the appropriate power balance between service and non-service committees was unresolved at the creation of UNISON and, as we shall see in later chapters, this provided an agenda to which many wished to speak within UNISON. This distinction between service and non-service groups was also to feature in UNISON's plans for oppressed social groups. It is to this agenda, that this chapter now turns.

In the interests of members: Part II

Although not central to the merger negotiations, considerable attention was paid to involving women and other oppressed social groups in the new union. From the start of the negotiations, all three unions accepted the principle of providing an effective approach to the representation of women (Terry, 1996). The strategies adopted in the rule book and Code of Good Branch Practice emanated from the work of a pre-merger Equal Opportunities Group. The group included four senior female paid officers and was informed by lay consultations and prevailing debates concerning gender democracy in wider society.

Prescriptions to address exclusion through domestic commitments

As noted in Chapter 1, the former partner unions already provided childcare facilities for members attending union business. UNISON provided another means of supporting members with dependants wishing to participate in unions. The rule book established the right to job-share branch positions. This rule was given more legitimacy in the Code of Good Branch Practice which noted that 'branches are required to give serious consideration' to making use of the job-share facility. In addition, prior to gaining approval as newly created UNISON branches, proposals were required to show how branches were considering the child/dependant-care responsibilities of members when determining the venue, timing and frequency of meetings.

Prescriptions for paid officers

As noted above, Kelly and Heery's (1994) argument that decentralisation could work to the detriment of marginalised groups does not appear to have underpinned arguments against branch autonomy or for partnership – and indeed were not alluded to in later debates of a similar nature. However, prescriptions to address the recruitment of under-represented groups and provide harassment-free environments were adopted – albeit outside of the rule book or at a later date.

A number of writers argue for strategies to recruit paid officers from under-represented groups, particularly women (Cunnison and Stageman, 1993; Kelly and Heery, 1994). This is of particular relevance to UNISON, which is male-dominated. Two years before merger, it is estimated that 48 per cent of COHSE national officers, 10 per cent of NALGO national officers and 33 per cent of NUPE national officers were women (Labour Research, 1994). At merger, this translated into approximately 20 per cent of national officers being women.

Strategies for recruitment, however, are unlikely to be found in the UNISON rule book since the usual 'rules of the game' are that the employment of paid officers is subject to union negotiations, rather than the membership rule book. This norm did not preclude an indication in the rule book that the first General Secretary of UNISON would be the General Secretary of NALGO as well as very detailed rules about the role of the NUPE and COHSE General Secretaries and Deputy General Secretaries. It did, however, exclude commitments to recruit from under-represented groups. In a similar vein, the rule book is silent on the employment of officers with responsibility for oppressed social groups. Prior to the merger, NALGO had employed women's officers in each region but this was not included in the rule book. Notwithstanding these omissions, UNISON officers did find a way of supporting paid officers from under-represented groups. The new union included an Organisation Development Unit, which established a Women's Development Project for achieving a balance between men and women officers (UNISON, 1998b; Wheeler, 2000). Likewise Regional Women's Officers were retained in the posts to which they had been appointed – although the stability of their positions was the subject of continual debate and rumour within the union.

The need for a harassment-free working environment was pursued through the rule book. The first UNISON rule book (1993) indicated that members would face disciplinary action if they committed any 'deliberate racist or sexist act'. At a later date, this was extended to include 'any act of discrimination or harassment on grounds of race, gender, marital status, sexuality, disability, age, creed or social class; or any other discriminatory conduct which is prejudicial to the Aims and Objects' of the union (1997a). Following pressure from activists at successive NDCs, this was specifically focused at UNISON's working environment. In 1997 an appendix was added to the rule book (1997a) which noted that UNISON employees had the right not to be harassed by UNISON members and set out a very detailed procedure for dealing with a complaint of harassment.

Prescriptions for representation by individuals of oppressed social groups

As noted above, NUPE and COHSE had a preference for reserving seats for women representatives. However, despite having high numbers of women members, neither union reserved seats in proportion to their female membership. The rule-book commitment to proportionality was therefore new to all of the unions and provided a new source of authority and influence for women.

Proportionality is defined in UNISON's rule book (1993) as the 'representation of women and men in fair proportion to the relevant number of female and male members comprising the electorate'. The introduction of proportionality in UNISON is a clear example of women being identified as individuals in a sex-category in order to overcome the historical deficit of women representatives (Cockburn, 1996). At the time of the merger, seats were not reserved for individuals of any other oppressed social group. However, the participation and representation of all members was explicitly encouraged by a concept called 'fair representation'. The rule book defines fair representation as

...the broad balance and representation of members of the electorate, taking into account such factors as the balance between part-time and full-time workers, manual and non-manual workers, different occupations, skills, qualifications, responsibilities, race, sexuality and disability. (UNISON, 1993, p. 65)

These rule-book commitments illustrate that the former partner unions were prepared to pursue a longer agenda of equal opportunities. However, as indicated in Chapters 4, 5 and 6, the rule book is the first step to providing authority and influence to oppressed social groups. Although proportionality and fair representation have the potential to challenge existing norms, this study shows how privileged groups could use the processes to their own advantage or could limit the potential of the challenge.

Prescriptions for oppressed social groups

Chapter 2 made a distinction between self-organisation and group representation. This indicated that self-organisation was a process for collective empowerment and reflective understanding of collective experiences and interests. In comparison, group representation was a process which provided oppressed social groups with the ability to either influence decisions (known as partial participation) or have equal power in determining the outcome of the decisions (known as full participation) (Pateman, 1970). Supporting self-organisation was seen as lengthening the agenda of equal opportunities in trade unions and group representation of oppressed social groups was seen as being the longest agenda.

Self-organisation   The extent of UNISON's support for self-organisation provided new sources of authority and influence to former NUPE and COHSE members and, to a certain extent, former NALGO members. Although NALGO had supported self-organisation, it was not on the scale pursued within UNISON. Women members, black members, members with disabilities and lesbian and gay members are all given opportunities to organise within self-organised groups (UNISON, 1993, pp. 19–20). Before discussing the details of this support, it is necessary to consider the particular case of women's self-organisation.

Cockburn (1996) argues for the representation of women as individuals of oppressed social groups *and* the representation of women as an oppressed social group. Although this strategy has been adopted by

UNISON, it must be noted that self-organisation for women was a late addition. During the merger negotiations, questions were raised as to the appropriateness of self-organisation for women in a female-dominated union aiming for proportionality by the year 2000. Indeed, whilst the final recommendations on the merger include provision for the other three groups, they omitted any provision for women's self-organised groups. Provision for women's self-organisation was only added at the insistence of the pre-merger NALGO Conference. As will be seen later, the concerns raised in this discourse were still apparent during the research.

The rule book gives self-organized groups opportunities to meet together to share concerns and aspirations, establish their own priorities, elect their own representatives, and generally work within a sufficiently flexible structure to build confidence and participation amongst members. In particular, self-organised groups have adequate and agreed funding and other resources (including education and training, access, publicity and communications) to operate at branch, regional and national levels. This funded and resourced structure appears to contain the key elements of autonomy cited by Briskin (1999): resource control, decision-making powers, and an organized and politicized constituency. However, a key feature to look at more closely is the location and constituency of the self-organized groups. It is also important to note that the reconciliation of self-organised groups with mainstream committees was a matter of unresolved balance and contest that carried into UNISON (Fryer, 2000).

Although members in UNISON are organised in service groups, the regional and national self-organised groups are organised along non-service group lines. Self-organised groups had access to cross-service regional and national structures but the rules did not provide self-organised groups with access to service groups at these levels. This means that it is only at branch level that self-organised groups can develop and pursue service specific concerns. Thus the collective experience at regional and national level is as members of a social group within UNISON, not as members of a social group working in, say Local Government. The non-service group nature of the self-organised groups is further underlined by the relationship between the self-organised groups and the mainstream committees. This can be analysed using the key elements suggested by Briskin (1999) – protective mandates for women's committees, union-wide communication potential, direct input into organisation decisions and links to the collective bargaining process. Whilst UNISON's rule book provides for the first two elements, it is less generous regarding the latter two elements, which raises questions about whether UNISON is supporting self-organisation or group representation.

Group representation?   The rule book provides self-organized groups with direct input into organizational decision making at branch, regional and national level.   The rules state that self-organized groups may formulate proposals, motions and other initiatives for the respective mainstream committees and conferences.   This is limited in two ways. The first limitation relates to Young's (1990) model of group representation that generates new sources of authority, influence and coercive power to oppressed groups.   In UNISON, decision makers are not obliged to take account of policies generated by the self-organised groups, nor do self-organised groups have veto power regarding specific policies that directly affect them.   Instead, the rule book reaffirms the need for self-organised groups to 'work within the established policies, rules and constitutional provisions of the Union' (UNISON, 1993, p.20). The National Delegate Conference provides an example of this limitation. Although the National Women's Conference may submit two motions to the NDC, there is no obligation on the Standing Orders Committee to prioritise these two motions.   In addition, although two representatives of each self-organised group at national level are entitled to attend the NDC and speak, they have no voting rights.

The second limitation relates to the location of the rights for group representation.   Although seats are reserved for self-organized group representatives on Regional Committees (UNISON, 1993, p. 28), this is a non-service group structure.   As noted above, the first rule book did not contain any links between self-organised groups and service groups, but the following section shows how it was possible to change this particular practice.

Initially, the point of contact between the SGEs and self-organised groups was through a liaison panel consisting of members of the SGE and chairs of the national self-organised groups.   The National Lesbian and Gay Members self-organised group (NLGG) sought two representative seats at the Local Government Service Group conference for each self-organised group.   Although excluded from submitting this motion themselves, they drafted a motion for adoption by the LGSG Executive. The motion was carried at the SG Conference and a rule change was agreed at the 1995 NDC to ensure that this representation was available at all Service Groups Conferences.   However, this does not mean that the union was prepared to adopt group representation across all levels of the union.   A motion seeking representation and participation of self-organised groups on national and regional service group committees was not prioritised and, therefore, not discussed. During 1996, the National Lesbian and Gay Conference submitted similar motions to individual service group conferences. The position adopted by the SGEs was to seek remittance of the motions, to oppose them, or in the case of the LGSG Executive, to submit their own amendment.

In 1996, the LGSG Conference voted to clarify and extend their relationship with self-organised groups. They agreed to timetable regular consultations with representatives of the self-organised groups, call upon regions to do likewise, continue to consult with groups on current negotiations around equal opportunities, and produce publicity for members in local government. This publicity was to provide 'practical advice and information, outlining issues affecting members from each self-organised group at work and a negotiation pack to improve working conditions'.   Again, however, although the union chose to extend consultation with the self-organised groups, at the same time, they rejected calls for a mechanism for representation on the national and regional service group committees from members of each self-organised group. They also rejected a campaign for increased finance to cover the cost of effective representation on these committees.

The detail of these changes has been included for two reasons: it illustrates the extent to which self-organisation is recognised as a legitimate entity within UNISON, but it also illustrates the boundaries of that legitimacy. This mixed picture of UNISON's pursuit of democracy for oppressed social groups is a reoccurring theme of this study.

Reshaping trade unionism?

As noted above, this study of UNISON provides a mixed picture of their ability to reshape and change dominant values of trade unionism. The extent to which UNISON has generated new sources of power for women should not be underplayed. By implementing proportionality in a female-dominated union, former sources of men's authority have been limited and new sources of authority have been generated for individual women. This could create greater sources of power if individual women act as a group since proportionality should ensure that they are the majority decision makers.   By implementing self-organisation for women, UNISON has maintained the source of authority that existed for women within the former partner unions. It has increased this authority through the granting of group representation rights to mainstream committees. By implementing women's self-organisation at the same time as proportionality, it has provided a potential link between new sources of authority for individual women and sources of new women for representative positions. Viewed in the context of other unions, UNISON has indeed changed some dominant values in trade unionism. However, in the context of the prescriptions for gender democracy outlined in Chapter 2, more could have changed.

A key limitation to this model of trade unionism is the lack of coercive power available to self-organised groups. Although they have been identified as an oppressed social group, they have not been given any source of power that would redress the imbalance between them and privileged groups. Although the power of self-organised groups could develop over time, it would have looked different if it had started from the desire to give power, influence and authority to women as an oppressed social group. There is sure to be a story to tell of how this mixed picture emerged but from available material it would appear that prominent groups mobilised bias for discussing the relationship between activists and paid officers rather than between privileged and oppressed social groups.

A telling illustration of this gender-neutral analysis is a report by Ouroussoff, conducted prior to the merger (1993). Despite being the result of a five-month study of the cultures of COHSE, NALGO and NUPE, women as a distinct category of individuals only enter the picture on the penultimate page, and then only in relation to a discussion of women officers, not women members. It should be noted that the issue of racial difference does not enter the discussion at all. The study of cultures focuses on the differing definitions of democracy within the partner unions. No doubt these definitions came from the members and officers themselves, but it is interesting to note that despite women comprising a significant proportion of the membership, the study lacks any gendered analysis. A gender-neutral analysis is unlikely to enable members to think the unthinkable. Whilst UNISON has taken an innovative step forward with its rule-book commitments to proportionality, fair representation and self-organisation, it has not taken the opportunity to move away from the traditional power structures of unions.

So, whose prescriptions are in the rule book? This chapter suggests that those with power vested in the structures of former partner unions have been most able to shape the rules of the game. Even so, not all issues were resolved at the creation of UNISON. Fryer (2000) noted that the balance between the centre and the regions, the relationship between officers and lay representatives, and the integration of self-organised groups and the mainstream were ongoing issues of contention. As we shall see in later chapters, these issues do not stand apart from the generation of new sources of authority for individual women.[1]

---

[1] This account has assumed that the pursuit of gender democracy has been limited because of other considerations. We cannot discount the possibility that future accounts of the merger negotiations may reveal the converse – that radical changes were achieved precisely because the primary focus was on other issues and equal opportunities could take large steps in the shadows.

4 Women Gaining Access

The rule-book prescriptions for proportionality and fair representation support the generation of new sources of authority for individual women as they gain access to representative structures. Using material collected from the constitutions and elections of five mainstream committees, this chapter identifies how these new sources of authority evolved post-merger and how they altered the political process for men and women.

UNISON is a new union and although the rule book covers many elements of democracy, it is silent on a number of issues. Some relate to the unresolved issues noted in Chapter 3, some provide an element of autonomy for service and non-service groups. As a consequence, the representative structures of the NEC are the closest indication in the rule book of what a representative structure should look like when proportionality and fair representation are being adopted. During the first years of UNISON, there was much scope for the negotiation of a new reality at different levels of the union. Material was collected from structures and elections of the National Executive Council (NEC), Health Care Service Group Executive (HCSGE), Local Government Service Group Executive (LGSGE) and two regions (denoted Region 1 and Region 2 for the purposes of this study). With the exception of the NEC, I attended decision-making bodies in all of these governing structures and interviewed activists and officers associated with all five. As this chapter will illustrate, the creation of new representative structures provided opportunities for activists and officers to mobilise bias for or against particular democratic practices. All of these democracy debates had implications for the representation of women – although not all of them explicitly noted this.

This chapter begins by describing the structure of the NEC and indicating how UNISON's first NEC election almost achieved proportionality. This result is then compared with the first elections of two service groups and two non-service group committees. Although all four committees sought to achieve proportionality and fair representation, only two did. Detailed study of the committees indicates the manner in which officers and activists were filling the silence of the rule book and thereby limiting or extending the representation of members in general and women in particular.

The chapter isolates four sets of decisions (and non-decisions) that had implications for the operation of proportionality and fair representation. These sets concerned the use of multi-representative constituencies, the balloting process, the quantity of seats reserved for low paid women and the filling of vacant seats. Some decisions had already been made at the time of the research, others were made in conferences and committees I attended. Each set of decisions shows how activists and officers attempted to make and shape the rules.

Identifying women as individuals in a sex-category: the NEC structure

Proportionality is the representation of women and men in fair proportion to the relevant number of female and male members comprising the electorate. The electorate for the NEC is the membership of UNISON. At the time of its creation, two-thirds of UNISON's membership were women. To meet this rule, a structure and electoral process was required which would produce an NEC consisting of at least 67 per cent women. As noted in Chapter 2, two key elements of increasing the election of women to representative structures are the reservation of seats for women in multi-representative constituencies.

At the creation of UNISON, every member belonged to one of seven service groups and one of 13 regions and the NEC consisted of representatives from each of the service groups and regions. Thus there were a total of 20 separate constituencies electing members to the NEC. Each constituency was allocated more than one representative. This meant that at least one, or more, of the representatives could be a woman.

Four categories of seats were created to provide multi-representative constituencies. Two categories were designed for members of a specific sex-category: men's seats and women's seats. One category was designed for members of a sex-category and an economic group: low-paid women's seats. At the time of the first NEC election, the candidacy for low-paid women's seats was restricted by rule to 'female members earning less than the maximum of the lowest subscription band set out in

Schedule A' – at that time £5,000. The fourth category could be contested by men, women or low-paid women and was denoted a 'general seat'. Once the exact membership of each region and service group was determined, the NEC consisted of 61 seats – the breakdown of which is contained in Table 4.1. As the figures in Table 4.1 indicate, the reservation of sex-categorised seats within multi-representative constituencies provides a framework for including women (and excluding men) in proportion to their membership of the electorate. The potential for this framework to facilitate proportionality in practice is indicated by the election results for the first NEC. These results are contained in Figure 4.1.

Figure 4.1 presents data on the total number of seats taken: 56. Women occupy 35 (62 per cent) of these seats. This equates to the minimum number of seats designated for women (62 per cent). Although proportionality (that is, 67 per cent) was not quite achieved at the first NEC election, this election result did provide a new source of authority for individual women from within the former partner unions.

In 1991, female membership of the former partner unions was 79 per cent in COHSE, 55 per cent in NALGO and 75 per cent in NUPE (Labour Research, 1994). In the same year, the executive committees of the former partner unions comprised 54 per cent women in COHSE, 50 per cent women in NALGO and 42 per cent women in NUPE. These figures demonstrate the extent to which proportionality and fair representation brought extra women onto the NEC.

The distance between women's representation on the first NEC (62 per cent) and the maximum possible representation by women (75 per cent) reflects the low number of women contesting general seats and the number of low-paid women's seats left vacant – features discussed in further detail below.

With regard to the lower paid seats, 9 of 13 low-paid women's seats were filled. The four vacant seats lower the proportion of low-paid women on the NEC, at the same time as lowering the proportion of women *per se* on the NEC. The next section emphasises the importance of multi-representative constituencies to the achievement of proportionality.

Table 4.1   Allocation of seats on NEC

Category of seat	Service group	Regional
Women's seat	2 Local Government 2 Health Care 1 Higher Education 1 Gas	2 in 6 regions* 1 in 7 regions*
Men's seat	1 Local Government 1 Health Care	1 in all 13 regions
Low-paid women's seat	---	1 in all 13 regions
General seat	1 in all 7 service groups	1 in all 13 regions
BREAKDOWN OF SEATS	6 women's seats 2 men's seats 0 low-paid women's seats 7 general seats 15 service seats of which 6 (40 per cent) are reserved for women	19 women's seats 13 men's seats 13 low-paid women's seats 1 general seat 46 regional seats of which 32 (70 per cent) are reserved for women

BREAKDOWN OF ALL 61 SEATS

Minimum women representatives: 38 seats (62 per cent) Maximum men representatives: 23 seats (38 per cent)
Maximum women representatives: 46 seats (75 per cent) Minimum men representatives: 15 seats (25 per cent)

*determined by regional size

Figure 4.1   Results of the first NEC election*

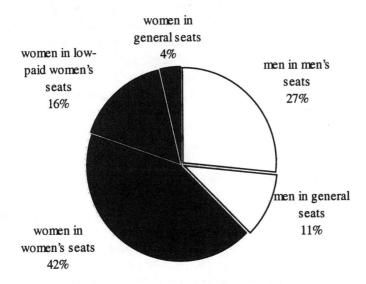

* This chart represents taken seats only, that is, 56 out of a possible 61.

The importance of multi-representative constituencies

The NEC adopted multi-representative constituencies for its structure, as did the service groups and regional groups. As noted earlier, this ensures that at least one seat can be reserved for a woman representative. However, this principle has not been applied to all committees and several very important committees retain single-representative constituencies. Those discussed below are the National Standing Orders Committee of the NDC, HCSGE sector committees and branch executive committees.

National Standing Orders Committee for the National Delegate Conference

The National Standing Orders Committee is responsible for determining the order in which the business of the National Delegate Conference (NDC) should be conducted. This responsibility includes accepting or rejecting conference motions, prioritising the order of conference business and determining the rules of conduct. Since the NDC is the sovereign decision-making body in the union, this committee plays an extremely important role in the union. The rule book states that the Standing Orders Committee should consist of a single-representative from each of the 13 regions and three members of the National Executive Council. Although the rule book provided a framework to ensure that the first Standing Orders Committee consisted of representatives from all three former partner unions, it was silent regarding the achievement of proportionality and fair representation.

Ensuring proportionality and fair representation amongst single-representative constitutions would require a systematic plan of action to which all regions agreed. However, regions elect their representatives in isolation of each other and it is not possible to ensure that significant numbers of the regional representatives are women. Using this single-representative structure, the majority of regions elected men to the 1994 Committee. Despite some of the NEC representatives being women, women were in the minority on the first NDC Standing Orders Committee (UNISON, 1994e). At the 1996 NDC, five of the thirteen regional posts were filled by women, and two of the three NEC seats were filled by women (UNISON, 1996a). That is, three years from the creation of UNISON, only 44 per cent of the committee were women.

So long as there is only one representative sent from each region, proportionality and fair representation will be difficult to achieve. Making this a multi-representative post would help, as would making it a mandatory job-share post, or arranging the rotation of the post between men and women over a period of time. However, all of these options have implications for the unresolved issue of power between the centre and the regions (Fryer, 2000). A motion to the 1995 NDC proposed that two regional representatives be appointed (at least one of whom would be a women) to the Standing Orders Committee. This was opposed by the NEC, was not prioritised for debate and was not debated. Perhaps this reflects a reluctance to increase regional representation on this national committee. In turn, regions are reluctant to give up their autonomy in choosing their own representative.

Health Care Service Group Executive sector committees

As noted in Chapter 3, sector committees comprise representatives from specific occupational groups within a larger service group (for example, admin and clerical workers within the health service). The service group is given the responsibility for deciding how these representatives will be indirectly elected to each sector committee. In Local Government, each sector committee developed a formula which, through the use of multi-representative constituencies and sex-categorisation of seats (women's seats, general seats and low-paid women's seats) provided that at least 44 per cent of representatives on each committee would be women. This was an important decision given that the sector committees in local government are directly involved in collective bargaining issues.

The HCSG Executive has eight sector committees and the interim executive committee decided that each sector group should comprise one representative from each region. In recognition of the fact that single-representative constituencies do not facilitate proportionality and fair representation, it was agreed that any sector committee should be entitled to co-opt up to five additional members. However, although these co-opted members would be entitled to speak, they would have no right to vote on the committee. When the structure of the sector committees was discussed at Conference, activists argued for two representatives to be elected from each region to facilitate proportionality in the sector committees. This argument was lost and, during my period of research, there was no mechanism for ensuring that women were elected to a minimum number of voting seats. Although sector committees in the HCSG are not involved in collective bargaining, this decision differs from that made by activists in the LGSG.

Branch Executive Committees

The branch provides a different set of challenges for those wishing to achieve proportionality and fair representation. Whereas all seats on service group and regional committees hold the same responsibilities, the posts on the branch Executive Committee have discrete and different roles (for example, Secretary, Chair, Treasurer, Welfare Officer, and Equality Officer). This means that although it is possible to job-share these posts, in practice only one representative post exists. In essence, since these jobs are not interchangeable, they produce single-representative constituencies that attract members wishing to hold a specific post. This provides a difficult context in which to reserve seats specifically for women – thereby facilitating proportionality. Just as important is the difficulty it raises for facilitating fair representation – an issue discussed in more detail in Chapter 6.

Comparing the NEC with other committee structures

The NEC was the only committee whose structure was detailed in the rule book and it provides a useful illustration of how proportionality and fair representation can be achieved. It also provides a template against which to compare structures and elections of other mainstream committees. The NEC results can be compared to the results of the first elections for the Local Government Service Group Executive, Health Care Service Group Executive, Regional Committee (Region 1), and Regional Committee (Region 2), presented in Figure 4.2.

Only two of these four committees achieved proportionality for elected seats – the Local Government Service Group Executive (LGSGE) and the Regional Committee in Region 2. In the LGSGE, 27 women were elected to 37 seats. This meant that women took 73 per cent of directly elected seats, which compares very favourably with the 65 per cent female electorate in the Local Government Service Group. The detailed study of these four committees, in the context of the NEC template, indicates three key features that affect proportionality: the balloting process, the quantity of low-paid women's seats, and post-election, the filling of vacant seats. The manner in which activists and officers shaped these particular features, thereby increasing or lessening the impact of proportionality and fair representation, is discussed below.

The balloting process

The structure of the NEC sets out very strong prescriptions for the reservation of sex-categorised seats. Although the sex-categorisation of seats facilitates proportionality and fair representation, it also requires that women make a choice about which seats to stand for – general seats, or women's seats. It also provides an opportunity for men and women to stand on a common agenda, or 'slate', across the general and women's seats.

Some activists saw this as an obstacle to women's increased access to representative structures and tried to adopt a different balloting system at a regional (non-service group) and service-group level.

Figure 4.2   Results of first elections in Local Government and Health Care Service Group Executives and Regional Committees in Regions 1 and 2*

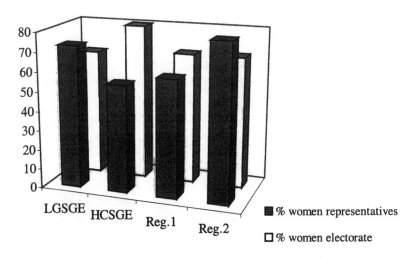

* This relates to directly elected seats on the LGSGE and HCSGE and regional representative seats on the Regional Committees. It excludes seats taken by representatives indirectly elected from other committees

Regional elections

Pre-merger regional guidelines indicated that each regional committee should consist of 20 regional representative seats. The guidelines suggested that these seats were split into eight general seats, eight women's seats and four low-paid women's seats and be supplemented by seats for each service group and seats for each self-organised group. Region 1 introduced this structure without change. With the exception of the low-paid women's seats which remained the same, Region 2 made the decision not to categorise seats as either women's or general seats. Interviews suggest that the initiative came from former NALGO women lay members who wanted a system that allowed for more women representatives, without creating women's seats.

Region 2 established a system whereby seats were not denoted as 'general' or 'women's' until after the election. Post-election, at least 50 per cent of those elected would be women. To achieve this objective, those candidates (men and women) attaining the eight highest votes took up general seats, and women candidates with the next eight highest votes took women's seats. Thus the sentiment of the national guidelines was upheld. Table 4.2 below illustrates the difference between the electoral process in the two regions.

Table 4.2   Allocation of regional representative seats in Regions 1 and 2

Region 1	*Region 2*
8 general seats	16 seats on single ballot of which
8 women's seats	at least 50% will be held by
	women
4 low-paid women's seats	4 low-paid women's seats
minimum women representatives:	minimum women representatives:
60% women	60% women
20% low-paid women	20% low-paid women

Excluding the low-paid women's seats, women candidates in Region 2 are not standing explicitly for either a general or women's seat, but 50 per cent of these women are guaranteed a seat. In 1994 and 1995, the single-ballot voting system in Region 2 produced a majority of women in the regional seats. In the 1994 election, four women won general seats. In the 1995 election, two women won general seats, thus producing 80 per cent and 70 per cent women in the regional seats respectively. This compares with no women being elected to general seats in Region 1. In the 1994 Region 1 election, 42 candidates contested eight general seats, and from information available, at least six of these candidates were women. In contrast, by the second election, the general seats only attracted 16 candidates, none of whom were women.

Activists in Region 2 argued that their electoral system enabled more women to get elected than a system involving separate lists for general and women's seats. Although fewer women were elected to general seats in the second election in Region 2, one interviewee noted that this was probably due to tactical voting in the election. Region 2 use a Single Transferable Voting (STV) system and she suggested that this could be manipulated against women obtaining general seats, by giving men the first-preference votes. Without looking into all the elections and studying the behaviour of a number of candidates and voters, it is difficult to prove that a single-ballot system is better than a separate-seat system. However, a single-ballot system does eliminate the need for women to choose between standing for a general or women's seat. This might be important if the mobilisation of bias was for general seats to be taken by men.

A regional committee member in Region 1 noted that she had not stood for a general seat, because it did not seem 'fair' to do so when women's seats existed. Thus, for this member, the general seats were implicitly 'men's seats'. However, she did note that she was thinking of standing for a general seat in the next regional committee elections. That general seats tended to be the preserve of men in Region 1 was illustrated by a figure of speech used during the election process. A number of different voting papers were circulated at the Annual General Meeting and there was great potential to create confusion amongst the delegates. To ease this confusion, the (female) Regional Convenor distinguished the voting papers for the general seats, by saying 'blue for the boys'. Given that no women had stood for general seats in this election, this was indeed the case, but the phase nonetheless underlined an evolving rule of the game. The difference between separate and single ballots is discussed below in relation to the service-group ballots. Before turning to service groups, however, it is worth comparing the actions of Regions 1 and 2 on another aspect related to proportionality.

Elections for regional seats on the Regional Committee are held at the Regional Council, so the make-up of the Regional Council is of relevance to the electoral process. Thus, whilst a minimum level of representation by women has been built into regional committees, the gender breakdown of the Regional Council is still of importance to the process of election.   Guidelines from the pre-merger regional constitutional working party stated:

> ...it has been agreed that each branch will be entitled to have one delegate per 1000 members or part thereof. Where branches are entitled to have more than one delegate at *least 50%* of their delegation must be women. (original emphasis)

Region 1 implemented this guideline, but its use precipitated considerable debate within the region. A Water Service Group branch applied for a waiving of the 50/50 ruling, arguing that the branch had far fewer women members. However, two appeals against the rule were refused, which was seen as quite a milestone in UNISON's development, and a success for women. Region 2 deviated in its interpretation of the national guidelines. Instead of suggesting that at least 50 per cent of delegations should be women, it asked that 'delegations should reflect proportionality in the branch'. A key figure in developing the constitution noted that a definite decision was made not to use a 50/50 rule as it could be used as a means of discriminating against men, and therefore fall into disrepute. In addition, this region felt that their definition was more in keeping with the original rule-book definition of proportionality. Therefore, had the Water branch been in Region 2 and not sent any women delegates, they would not necessarily have been challenged.

This digression has been included to provide a different interpretation of Region 2's action. In the first decision, activists are seen to be acting in the interests of women but this is not so obvious in the second decision. What is consistent across both decisions, however, is the rejection of the guidelines. It raises questions as to whether other motivations underpin these decisions. Another possibility is that activists were seeking to exert their autonomy from the national guidelines. One possibility is that former NALGO activists were ameliorating what they saw as the worst elements of reserved seats.

Service group ballots

Originally, elections to the HCSGE were to be through a single ballot, in which women would take at least 50 per cent of seats. At least one other service group (Higher Education) also proposed a single ballot for its SGE elections. However, the use of a single-ballot system for service groups did not materialise. The administration of the national service group elections was organised centrally within the union and interviewees suggest there was a strong push from officers for all service group elections to be administered in the same way. The use of separate lists of candidates for general and women's seats was the preferred option of the officers. Interviewees noted that officers argued that single ballots would require more explanation and would be difficult and off-putting for voters.

After discussion within the relevant lay committee of the interim NEC (the Administrative Panel), the decision was made that all national service group elections would use separate ballots for women's and general seats. The issue that the two systems might produce different nominations, and thereby different results, was apparently not addressed. Members commenting on the process referred to the 'bureaucratic' approach taken by (mostly male) officers. The issue was seen essentially as an administrative matter and a number of key groups were not consulted: the women's structure, the Organisation Development Panel of the NEC, and the Equal Opportunities Panel of the NEC. As expressed by one interviewee, the work on the administration of elections 'happened elsewhere'. A proponent of single-ballot papers noted that, in her opinion, this decision had 'put back the union 20 years'.

As noted above, the extent to which this decision changed women's access to representative structures is difficult to gauge. Women contested five of the 13 general seats on the HCSGE and won none of them. This contrasts with the LGSGE where women contested five of the 14 general seats and won four. If we assume that a single-ballot system makes no difference to candidate and voting behaviour, then the voting figures of the first HCSGE election suggest that a single ballot would not have made any difference to the number of women representatives elected to the SGE. However, interviews suggest that single ballots do make a difference to candidate behaviour. A HCSGE member who stood in a women's seat justified her decision by noting that there had only been one other member in the region who had indicated an intention to be nominated in the election. Since this other member was a man, it had seemed sensible for him to stand unopposed for the general seat, and for her to stand unopposed for the women's seat. She intimated that her actions might have been different had there been more nominations forthcoming. Other insights into the candidate and voting behaviour of activists are provided in Chapter 5.

Returning to the shaping of representative structures, a factor in the LGSGE achieving proportionality is the proportion of seats allocated to women. The following section indicates the critical contribution that low paid women's seats make to this total.

The contribution of low-paid women's seats to proportionality

As noted above, fair representation is facilitated on representative structures by the provision of seats for low-paid women. Because women occupy these seats, these seats also contribute to the achievement of proportionality. This is because the number of women's seats required for proportionality is inclusive, rather than exclusive, of low-paid women's seats. Thus, the relationship between low-paid women's seats and proportionality is an important one. This can be seen in the structure of the NEC (see Table 4.1 above). When a low-paid women's seat is allocated to each region, it ensures that 70 per cent of these NEC regional seats are available for women. When no low-paid women's seats are allocated to service groups, only 40 per cent of the NEC service-group seats are guaranteed for women.

Within the confines of the rule book, service groups were able to determine their own structures. Although they were required to take account of proportionality and fair representation, the rule book was silent on how this was to be achieved. Figure 4.2 indicates that the Local Government Service Group Executive achieved proportionality and the Health Care Service Group Executive did not. A key determinant of this outcome relates to the different manner in which activists and officers influenced the number of low-paid women's seats within each structure. The NEC structure had provided one low-paid woman's seat per region, but neither of these two service groups adopted this principle at the outset.

The Local Government Service Group Executive

The initial structure provided for one low-paid women's seat for each region that consisted of more than 50,000 Local Government Service Group members. Eight of the 13 regions met this criterion and, in common with the NEC, the candidacy of the seats was restricted to members earning less than £5,000. As noted earlier, this level is likely to facilitate representation by women who work in part-time or manual jobs. The proposed structure – which included eight low-paid women's seats – was put to the first Local Government Service Group Conference in 1994. A branch motion was put to Conference to increase the number of low-paid women's seats to one per region (making a total of 13 low-paid women's seats). The motion was submitted by an un-merged branch representing Administrative, Professional, Technical and Clerical Staff Group (APT&C). The motion condemned the structure proposed by the interim committee, arguing that 'this decision will disenfranchise a large number of low paid members in both manual/craft and APT&C groups.' Support for this motion was apparently overwhelming and the proposed structure was amended to allow for one low-paid women's seat per region. The implications for proportionality of increasing the number of low-paid women's seats can be seen in Table 4.3. The initial proposal would have resulted in a minimum female representation of 59 per cent of the committee. The addition of the low-paid seats provides a minimum female representation of 64 per cent.

However, whilst the argument for increasing the number of low-paid women's seats could be viewed as a victory for women's representation, increasing the number of seats in a constituency can simultaneously increase the representation of other groups. In this case, increasing the number of low-paid women's seats automatically increased representation for five regions. The amendment was also likely to increase the representation of manual members, part-time members, former NUPE members and members within particular political factions. It would be inaccurate, therefore, to say that this increase was stimulated by a desire to increase the representation of women *per se*. Interviews and observations suggest that it could be variously attributed to a desire to increase representation by manual, low-paid women workers, to a reassertion of the balance of power between the centre and regions and to increase the power of lay representatives in relation to officers. The manner in which low-paid women's seats developed within the LGSG provides a strong contrast with the experience of the HCSG.

Health Care Service Group Executive

The interim Health Care Service Group Executive developed a structure that initially included four low-paid women's seats. Unlike the low-paid women's seats on the LGSGE, which were allocated according to regional size, these were allocated to four constituencies of geographically grouped regions. Again, these seats were reserved for women earning less than £5,000. The Service Group structure was formally moved at the first Health Care conference. The argument was voiced that four low-paid women's seats were not enough for the Executive. However, unlike the Local Government Service Group Conference, there were no formal motions to change the structure at this point. Since this time, there has been considerable debate about the number of low-paid women's seats on the HCSGE which provides a useful insight into the perceived nature of low paid women's seats and proportionality.

The agenda of the second HCSG Conference contained a motion that returned to this issue. The motion recognised the invaluable role played by low-paid women members and proposed that one low-paid women's seat should be allocated to each of the 13 regions. This motion therefore sought to increase the representation of low-paid women from four to 13. The motion added that the decision was to be effective from the current SGE elections. The policy of the interim SGE was to oppose this motion. A woman moved the motion and a male National Officer spoke against the motion on behalf of the interim SGE. The Officer argued that if Conference passed this motion, then voting would be void on the current SGE elections. This was guaranteed to be off-putting, since voting for the first substantive committee was currently underway. Reference was also made to the cost of creating nine extra seats on the committee. The motion went to a card vote and was defeated by 60 per cent of Conference.

This decision provides a stark contrast to the decision taken by the Local Government Service Group Conference. In the LGSG, increasing the number of low-paid women's seats was viewed as an opportunity to increase the representation of regions, manual members, part-time members, former NUPE members and members within political factions. Voters within the HCSG do not appear to have taken this view. Instead, the decision could be regarded as a vote to minimise representation by women in general, regions, and part-time and manual women workers.

One month after this conference decision, a low-paid woman member of the SGE asked if low-paid women could be mandated by each of the regions they represented. This question had arisen because the representative had been told that she should have voted in a particular way on a crucial vote about industrial action. Since the member represented three regions, she asked on a subsequent occasion whether she should have a vote for each region (that is, three votes). This question prompted a noticeable intake of breath around the room. At this point, the lead Officer of the Group said that it had never been intended that these women would be required to represent the grouped regions. Instead, he noted that providing low-paid women's seats on a multi-regional basis was a way of getting numbers of low-paid women onto the committee and enabling their voice to be heard. The debate continued over a period of time to a position whereby the SGE decided to allocate one low-paid women's seat per region.

Table 4.3   Allocation of directly elected seats in service groups

Local Government Service Group Executive	*Health Care Service Group Executive*
Women in electorate: 65%	Women in electorate: 80%
Proposed structure:	Proposed structure:
14 general seats 12 women's seats 8 low paid women's seats	13 general seats 13 women's seats 4 low paid women's seats
Minimum filled seats: 59% (inclusive of low-paid women)	Minimum filled seats: 56% (inclusive of low-paid women)
1st Conference: Proposal for amendment accepted:	1st Conference No proposal for amendment:
14 general seats 12 women's seats 13 low paid-women's seats	2nd Conference Proposal to increase number of low-paid women's seats rejected by 60% of conference
Minimum filled seats: 64% (inclusive of low-paid women)	Minimum filled seats: 56% (inclusive of low-paid women)

However, on this proposal being put to the SGE for approval, a male Executive member put forward an amendment to the effect that the allocation of one low-paid women's seat per region should be accompanied by the redesignation of general seats to men's seats. The member argued that this redesignation would be 'in the interests of proportionality', since each region would then have two women's seats, and one men's seat (that is, two-thirds female representation). He argued that this proposal would be in keeping with the use of men's seats on the NEC. This proposal prompted a lengthy debate about the issue during which there was no observable gender split between opinions. Significant numbers of women were generally in agreement with the proposal to redesignate the general seats with only one woman lay member and one woman official explicitly objecting to the change.

The low-paid member who had originally raised the question noted that the issue was not about proportionality and that it had come about because she represented three regions but was not able to be mandated by each region.   After considerable debate the Health Care Group approached the National Women's Officer for constitutional advice. The National Women's Officer advised that if the structure were amended to provide two women's seats and one man's seat per region this would be contrary to the principle of proportionality. This argument was based on the constituency of the Health Care electorate, rather than the constituency of the wider union. She noted that since women comprise 80 per cent of the Health Care Group electorate, proportionality in this group meant that women should attain 80 per cent of executive seats, not 67 per cent as suggested by the proposed amendment.

The debate was resumed in a subsequent meeting – during which some men indicated that the absence of men's seats could mean that 'there might not be any men left on this committee.' This would suggest by this time, that these particular men were seeing women's increased access to the committee as being at their expense.   At the end of the debate the Committee voted to allocate one low-paid women's seat per region, and left the designation of the general seat unchanged. The SGE put this structure to the next Service Group Conference, which was duly passed by the delegates. Under the amended structure, 26 out of 39 directly elected seats (67 per cent) are designated for women – of which 13 are designated as low-paid women's seats. Although this minimum is some distance from the 80 per cent figure, it is higher than the proportion of seats originally proposed (56 per cent). A key difference between this structure and the proposal for men's seats is that women are able to increase their representation if they contest and win general seats. If these had been redesignated as men's seats, women's representation would have been capped at 67 per cent, as opposed to having no limit at present.

If the provision of low-paid women's seats in each region on the NEC is taken as a prescription for proportionality and fair representation, then comparison with the LG and HC service groups indicates a degree of resistance to this ideal. In particular, officers in both service groups resisted the allocation of one seat per region. The LG group allocated low-paid seats to the largest regions, and the HC group allocated low-paid seats to grouped regions. In the former case, this resistance was overcome by a strong pull from male and female activists to create more opportunities for regional representation by women who would definitely be low paid and who might also be manual workers and former NUPE members. In this case, it could be argued that privileged groups were making key decisions that favoured the oppressed social group of low-paid women. This is especially important given the lack of formal input into these discussions by women's self-organised groups. In the case of the HCSGE, male and female activists joined with officers to block proposed increases in regional representation. In this respect, this was a privileged group that was not taking the interests of an oppressed social group into consideration. However, officers of the HCSGE and the majority of activists did change their strategy at a later date to reflect the advice of the National Women's Officer. In the absence of formal input from the women's self-organised groups, this intervention by the paid officer was extremely important.

The previous sections have indicated how various groups took the opportunity to limit or extend the potential of proportionality when developing representative structures for the first time. The following section refers to the manner in which activists tried to influence proportionality and fair representation post-election.

Re-elections for vacant seats

Eight seats attracted no candidates in the first round of national service group elections. Since these were all women's seats, their empty state had an adverse effect on the extent to which proportionality was achieved. The debate as to whether new elections could be held for vacant seats was held in a number of national committees and I was present when it was discussed in the Health Care Service Group Executive. At the time of this discussion, their structure allocated low-paid women's seats to four grouped regions. Observation of the debate illustrates how certain members of the committee were mobilising bias against filling the seats.

First, the debate took place at the end of the meeting, at the end of the day, when fewer people were present, including only one low-paid woman. Second, at the commencement of the debate, the National Officer noted that not filling the vacant seats would mean one less low-paid woman on the HCSGE but that holding a health election over three or four regions for the low-paid seat would incur a cost. Third, after some debate, a senior activist put forward her view 'as a member of the Administration and Finance Panel on the NEC'. She stated that the vacant seats should not be filled because of the cost. She argued that since they did not get nominations the first time the money should not be spent on seeking new nominations and proposed that the seat should remain vacant.

At this point, some members noted that the discussions were not acknowledging the difficulty of representation for low-paid women – particularly when they represented grouped regions. A proposal to fill the vacant seat was put to the vote and was passed by twelve votes to nine. The twelve men were split 50:50 on the motion and the nine women were split 2:1 in favour of filling the seat. Following this decision, nominations were sought for the low-paid women's seat and following the receipt of only one nomination, a woman was elected unopposed to this seat (thus incurring no additional cost).

Reference has been made to the effect of vacant seats on proportionality, so it is possible to construe the actions of the paid and lay officers of the Executive as a resistance to proportionality. It is also interesting that the issue of cost was brought into the discussion because this was the original argument against increasing the number of low-paid women's seats on the Health Care SGE. An interview with a (male) member of the Administration and Finance Panel of the NEC indicated that a number of people were less than interested in the reasons for vacant seats and were 'not keen on proportionality anyway':

Arguments were made that it gave women a second opportunity to get elected. This showed a lack of understanding of proportionality. It shows an insensitivity which comes from insecurity and lack of understanding of formalities, the reality of why there are vacant seats and the imbalance of opportunity for women.

Summary and discussion

The commitments to proportionality and fair representation in UNISON's rule book are an acceptance that not all members are equal and that women and low-paid women ought to be identified as distinct categories of members in order to increase their opportunities to be elected as representatives. This chapter has shown that proportionality can increase women's access to representative seats. The identification of women as a distinct group of members has enabled women's systematic inclusion within UNISON and some dramatic increases in women's access to the decision-making arena. Systematic inclusion has replaced the systematic exclusion of women that has been found in earlier studies. That is, it has been possible to change the rules of the game and generate new sources of authority for individual women that, in turn, have altered the political process of representation.

The manner in which proportionality and fair representation have been implemented provides us with insights into the shaping of dominant values within UNISON. In particular, it demonstrates how activists and officers mobilised bias for and against the expansion of representation. Paid officers, supported by some senior activists, argued against the use of multi-representative constituencies on the sector committees; they argued against the expansion of low-paid women's seats and against the filling of vacant seats. Kelly and Heery (1994) argue that paid officers deploy a range of choices at their own discretion and this chapter suggests that a number of officers within UNISON were choosing to limit the representation of women. If this were the case, then partnership with these officers would not be in the interests of oppressed social groups.

With the exception of the debate over national balloting procedures, activists won all the arguments for increasing women's representation. Thus, on these issues, activists were able to shape the dominant values of UNISON to the advantage of women. However, as noted earlier, it would be inaccurate to suggest that activists are working wholly for the cause of women. An increase in women's representation provides an increase in representation *per se*. As noted in Chapter 3, the primary focus of merger negotiations was the relationship between lay activists and paid officers. Increasing women's representation could provide important sources of authority to rebalance relationships between the centre and the regions and between lay representatives and paid officers. The argument that new forms of authority for women have been supported because they benefit others is one of the themes discussed in the next chapter.

5 Taking Part in the Electoral Process

The previous chapter showed how rule-book commitments to proportionality and fair representation generated new sources of authority for women in representative structures in UNISON. It also illustrated how different groups of activists and officers were able to influence the potential of these new sources of authority. This chapter turns to the electoral processes themselves and indicates the responses of individuals and groups to the new sources of power. It deals with four main issues.

First, it illustrates the political opportunities that multi-representative constituencies create for groups within unions. Second, it examines the electoral activity of women who were already active in the former partner unions. Third, it indicates the manner in which proportionality and fair representation encourages new women to be pulled and pushed into representative structures. Fourth, it indicates how women were acting collectively to take up new seats. This analysis shows how groups already active in the political process were able to take advantage of the new sources of authority generated for individual women. The chapter concludes that whilst proportionality and fair representation facilitated an increase in the number of individual women taking up representative seats, the need to gain representation for women as an oppressed social group still remains.

Political opportunities of multi-representative constituencies

The previous chapter showed the vital role that multi-representative constituencies play in facilitating proportionality and fair representation. It also showed how multi-representative constituencies could provide regions with more authority in relation to central administration and provide lay activists with more authority in relation to officers. This chapter illustrates the opportunities that multi-representative constituencies provide for organised groups to stand for election across all representative seats in the constituency. A 'slate' is the term used to indicate that a number of individuals are standing for election on a common agenda. A comparison was made in Chapter 4 between sex-categorisation of seats pre-election and post-election. The use of pre-election separate seats in multi-representative constituencies enabled organised groups to operate slates across a number of identifiable seats, thereby increasing their potential to retain or gain representational power.

The important issue for gender democracy is that proportionality and fair representation ensured that, where they operated, each slate needed to include at least one woman (for the women's seat) and one low-paid woman (for the low-paid women's seat). As indicated below, this had an immediate effect of pulling and pushing women into representative structures. A second effect was found in those structures that provided for three seats: a general seat, a women's seat and a low-paid women's seat. In this context, the women's seat was considered pivotal to gaining power within the union. This was illustrated most graphically in relation to the balance between former partner unions, although the same principle can be applied to power struggles between political groupings too.

Using the NEC as an example, a branch secretary outlined the perception that general or men's seats were virtually guaranteed to go to a former NALGO man and that low-paid women's seats were virtually guaranteed to go to former NUPE women. Assuming that this happened across most regions, a balance of power would be created between those seats held by former NALGO members and those occupied by former NUPE members. It was assumed, therefore, that the occupants of the women's seats would decide the power balance between the two groupings since they would be automatically creating a majority of 2:1 for their former partner union. (It is noteworthy that COHSE was not considered in this scenario.) Added to the perception that the women's seats could be won by women of any partner union, this strengthened incentives for women to retain or gain representative positions.

Electoral activity of existing women activists

The Local Government and Health Care service groups were each allocated four representative seats on the NEC: two women's seats, one men's seat and one general seat. Women in both service groups therefore had a choice of whether to stand for the women's seats or the general seat. An interview with an experienced woman activist who stood for one of these service-group seats demonstrates how women's seats were seen as an important part of an electoral slate.

The member noted that she had always been opposed to reserved seats but it was her perception that there was less competition for women's seats. In her opinion it seemed logical to stand for a women's seat, where she believed she would stand a better chance of getting elected. Seemingly nothing would have prompted her to stand for a general seat as she felt this seat would provide the least chance of being elected. In the event, this interviewee did not win one of the women's seats. She did, however, win a women's seat on her national SGE – again, choosing that seat because she felt it offered her the best chance of getting elected. The use of these group-based tactics was confirmed by another interviewee who noted that before the NEC election she and others would discuss the general and women's seats to see which was the best way of getting a seat on the NEC.

Such motivations did not go unnoticed by women members who argued that experienced women should only stand for general seats. First, because experienced women were deemed more able to win general seats. Second, because if experienced women won the women's seats, they were perceived as blocking access to newer active women. Third, because some of these experienced activists were not perceived as having pursued women's concerns in the past. However, as the following example illustrates, experienced women could be condemned for running for general seats too.

A male interviewee informed me how one woman's insistence on standing for a general seat, rather than a women's seat, meant that the union 'lost a very good person' when she won the seat over a male competitor. It was felt to be unfair by the interviewee and some of his colleagues that this woman – who had the opportunity to win one of three seats (that is, two women's seats, one general seat) – chose the process that potentially blocked one of the man's two opportunities, which were one men's seat and one general seat. Expectations of experienced women activists, and their activity, is a theme repeated in later chapters. The next section describes how new activists were pulled and pushed into representative positions.

Pulling and pushing women into representative positions

I have used the concept of 'pulling' women into representative positions to denote those situations where new women were encouraged to put themselves forward for election by individuals and groups already holding representative positions. One interviewee noted that when a department convenor was looking to stand down, the 'men controlling the branch were looking for a woman to fulfill their needs for proportionality'. The interviewee described how the men had approached her:

> I spoke at a Housing Department members' meeting and gave a well-received speech. The branch secretary and chair said they thought I would be good as convenor and thought I should be nominated. They asked me how I would receive that. It did seem daunting and I suspect it is for that reason that I was nominated. I do feel that it was because I was inexperienced that I was nominated. I think they fear losing control, as Housing is one of the biggest departments in Council and is politically active.

The possibility that women were being 'used' to achieve someone else's agenda was articulated by another member:

> I have been asked to be on everyone's slate. Everyone has a hole for a low-paid woman. These propositions were the first time I had heard of a slate and I wanted to ask what one was. I was told that 'we don't want any mavericks' – which I also wanted to know the meaning of. I'm annoyed that members are standing on slates. It is not a good way forward, particularly if it is along former union lines. I agree that women's seats are seen as useful in the battle for power, but not only between former partner unions, but between 'right and left' too. I was originally contacted by all quarters because of people's perceptions of my politics – they may be left, but not all the time on all issues. I made a verbal attack on the actions of the region after which 'the left' thought I was wonderful and wanted me to join up with them.

One of these interviewees noted how she dealt with such sponsorship at branch level:

> At first when they thought I was manipulable I got a lot of support – the 'come to the pub with us' thing. But since I've developed my own support I'm not getting the same treatment. Initially I relied on them too much and

asked them before I did anything. I don't do that now and there is more respect between us now.

The concept of 'pushing' women into representative positions denotes those situations where new women were encouraged to put themselves forward for election by officers and activists outside the representative structures. One member who was active at branch and regional level noted how she was persuaded to stand for a national seat:

> The full-time officer and convenor persuaded me to stand, as did NEC members from the region. I got a lot of support as I was well known in the region.

The involvement of paid officers in encouraging certain activists to stand is highly contentious and confirms some activists' fears that proportionality was a means of marginalising politically active members of the union. These concerns are clearly articulated in the following interview extracts:

> Officers are using proportionality and fair representation as a weapon to get their own way and imposing their policies.

> The reason proportionality was adopted wholeheartedly is that people saw it as a way of controlling the NEC. Women were assumed to be less articulate, and I'm pleased to see that this has proved to be wrong.

I am aware that the concept of pulling and pushing women into representative positions infers that women are the subjects of another's agenda. These observations suggest that when women are pulled or pushed into representative positions it is usually to ensure that existing representatives, or officers, retain or strengthen their power – a theme to which we return in later chapters. At the time of this research I found few examples of women entering the electoral process to increase the representation of women as a group. Examples of women organising themselves in the election process were found outside, rather than inside, formally instituted self-organised groups. For example, fears that the concerns of low-paid Local Government members would not be addressed without their presence underpinned these intentions of collective activity:

> I have never stood for a national seat before. Myself and [work colleague] felt we should do something. She went for the women's seat and I went for the low-paid women's seat.

> There are a number of women from school meals/cleaning who have been affected by CCT and motivated to become active. When your job is threatened you see the point of being there – it's about getting a voice for part-time workers and not getting overlooked.

The limited use by women acting as a group to the new sources of authority could be explained by the timing of my research. A paid officer reflected on the first SGE elections and told me that he thought women would be networking in the future:

> Women were not going for general seats because there was no slate. There are a number of strong activist women but none knew each other and they stood against each other. If [activist] had stood for the general seat, she may well have won it and then [activist] would have been able to take the women's seat. A slate is seen as a dirty word whereas networking is seen as an acceptable word. I think women will be networking in the future.

More recently, Colgan and Ledwith refer to organised electoral activity amongst self-organised groups. Two women and one man stood on a slate 'explicitly supporting UNISON's equality policies'. All four self-organised groups and others 'favouring culture change in the region' supported them. The desire for the oppressed social groups to take advantage of the new sources of authority generated for women is a clear objective of their activity:

> One of the women admitted that she had to think 'long and hard' before standing but had thought it was important that she had stood and been elected in order to give 'a very big confidence boost to self-organisation' and 'combat forces' in the region hostile to it. (Regional Convenor and SOG National and Regional Committee Member, Interview, November 1997) (Colgan and Ledwith, 2000, p. 253)

Summary and discussion

By creating a legitimate space for women, proportionality encourages a 'push and pull' effect on women's participation in representative structures. In a union in which women are the majority, proportionality means limiting the presence of men in proportion to their membership. In the past, without this restriction, the greater propensity of men to put themselves forward for representative positions led to more men being elected to lay positions. With men's activity being restricted, members are looking for women in order that proportionality can be achieved. When exercised by current representatives, this could be referred to as a 'pull' effect, and mirrors men being chosen for representative positions, in earlier studies. When exercised by non-representatives, this could be referred to as the 'push' effect. Again, the restriction on men's activity and the creation of legitimate spaces for women has created an environment that is more likely to encourage women to consider such activity. In these ways, it can be said that the 'rules of the game' have been changed.

Proportionality and fair representation provide individual women with new sources of authority and the last two chapters have shown how individuals and groups can shape the generation of these sources. These activities have occurred in two time periods. First, the values and beliefs of members and officers, men and women have informed the constitutions themselves. Secondly, the impact of these new constitutions has been realised through the responses of members and officers. In particular this chapter has illustrated the manner in which the interests and identities of women interact and produce a number of tensions and contradictions. Some women are keen for more women to be elected, but do not expect elected women to speak on women's concerns. Some women believe in increasing women's representation but only stand for women's seats. Some women do not believe that women should be identified for the purposes of representation, but are willing to use the system to get elected. Proportionality identifies women as members of a group and yet, as this chapter has shown, women act as individuals and as members of sub-groups that cut across gender. This in itself should not be a surprise but raises questions about the nature of the relationship between women representatives and the pursuit of women's concerns. It also focuses attention on the potential for links between women in mainstream committees and those in women-only groups. These issues are discussed in later chapters. The next chapter discusses the implementation of fair representation.

6 Fair Representation and Diversity

Fair representation is intended to encourage the representation of the broad balance of members of the electorate. The previous two chapters have indicated how the combination of fair representation and proportionality has facilitated women's access to representative structures. Chapter 4 showed how fair representation was pursued through low-paid women's seats. This had two consequences. First, although low-paid women's seats provided some class and occupation-based diversity amongst women, it did not address differences based on race, sexuality and disability – three features of fair representation noted in the rule book. Second, the pursuit of fair representation through women's seats left the diversity of men untouched by institutional mechanisms. The previous chapters have argued that privileged groups (including individual women) were more likely to seize the opportunities provided by the institutional mechanisms of proportionality than were members of oppressed social groups. This chapter examines the manner in which different groups sought to take advantage of the broader principles of fair representation. It addresses specific issues of class, race and gender.

First, it indicates how low-paid seats facilitate diversity amongst women but not amongst men. Second, it notes how some groups used the concept of fair representation to argue for more class-based and job-based diversity. These arguments found expression in strong pressures to reconceptualise fair representation in terms of a balance between former partner unions. Third, it indicates the absence of race, sexuality and disability in such discussions and illustrates the danger of prioritising gender and class-based fair representation over race. Fourth, it indicates how self-organised groups argued for the representation of their groups on the National Executive Council (NEC) and other bodies. Finally, the chapter reviews the arguments for and against reserved seats.

Diversity amongst women

It is important to remember that the creation of UNISON brought together a very wide cross-section of employees. The desire that all members should be equally represented – regardless of occupation – is given force by the rule book which notes that structures of representation should take into account 'the balance between part-time and full-time workers, manual and non-manual workers, different occupations, skills, qualifications, responsibilities, race, sexuality and disability'. As noted in Chapter 4, this rule has been pursued through low-paid women's seats. Such seats have been created on the NEC, national service group executives and regional committees. By restricting the candidacy of these seats to women earning less than £5,000, it was likely that these seats would be taken by women working part-time in manual jobs, thereby fulfilling at least six of the criteria. However, whilst this has enabled some job-based diversity amongst women representatives, men have been unaffected by such processes. This raised concerns that male manual workers were becoming excluded from representative structures and created resentment against proportionality which was seen as protecting white-collar women workers at the expense of male manual workers.

The structures outlined in Chapter 4 indicate that, with the exception of men's seats on the NEC, all male representatives had to compete with each other, and with women, for general seats. In this context, male manual and craft members were likely to be competing with male and female Administrative, Professional, Technical and Clerical (APT&C) members for general seats. In the Local Government Service Group Executive elections, three former male members of the Manual & Craft national sector committee lost to two men and one woman on APT&C terms and conditions. No male manual members won a directly elected seat on the first LGSGE. Approximately one-third of the first national SGE were members on Manual and Craft terms but only one was a man. This male manual worker was present because the Manual and Craft Sector Committee indirectly elected him to the SGE. This was a considerable change from previous committees within NUPE and emphasises the manner in which fair representation was pursued through women's seats. Low-paid women were gaining new sources of authority and influence on UNISON's national executive committee but this was at the expense of manual men who were losing the authority and influence that they held in their former union. Since women have the greater share of the total number of seats, the pursuit of fair representation through women's seats is understandable, but has implications for the future of the union if similar diversity is not attained amongst male activists. In the short term, it had implications for the manner in which significant numbers within the union interpreted fair representation.

Demands for class-based and job-based diversity

The creation of UNISON in Local Government brought senior managers and supervisors under the same organising umbrella as craft and manual workers. As noted by Fryer (2000), the recent past had seen managers planning job cuts or reorganisations that adversely affected manual workers. The bringing together of all Local Governments workers in the same union was a double-edged sword. On the one hand it would enable UNISON to have the greater say in the proposed single-status bargaining structures. On the other hand, it was viewed with suspicion and a fear that white-collar members would determine the terms and conditions of manual workers. Thus, for a significant proportion of members, class-based or job-based diversity was a key element of fair representation.

Although low-paid seats provided a degree of job-based diversity amongst the women, because of the earnings limit of £5,000, they were mostly likely to be filled by women who worked part-time. In UNISON, full-time women manual workers were now competing for women's seats with women on APT&C terms and conditions, or were contesting general seats with APT&C members. In the LGSGE elections, two former members of the Manual & Craft national Sector Committee lost to women on APT&C terms and conditions. Such results at national and local level left women manual members feeling that proportionality was being pursued at the expense of fair representation:

> I fully support proportionality but we have to ensure that every area of membership is protected. There is no self-protection for traditional manual workers. (female branch Secretary from an un-merged former NUPE branch)

> Twenty-five per cent of the regional committee are manual workers. The gender division is okay. Twenty per cent of the committee are health workers and the rest are APT&C. The convenors are also APT&C. When I

found this out, I wanted to jack it in at that point. (female manual worker, active at local, regional and national levels)

Local Government manual workers were not the only members who felt excluded within the new union. Health service workers also felt excluded – particularly at regional level. Although any member in the region can be nominated for election to the Regional Committee, only the delegates attending the AGM of the Regional Council can vote for the candidates. Although indirect elections are likely to perpetuate any bias of membership in the lower committee, this should not be the case at regional level since each branch is allowed to send at least one delegate to the Regional Council. However, being *entitled* to attend and being *able* to attend was seen as an important distinction.

The Regional Health Committee in Region 2 noted that a number of health service branches were unable to come to the Council to vote. This form of indirect election was criticised by the Regional Health Committee as creating a bias against health service workers. The Regional Health Committee proposed the direct election of Regional Committee representatives by all members in the region – not just those attending the Regional Council. Delegates supporting the proposed amendment argued for fairness, a widening of democracy, and an appreciation that 'health workers work seven days a week', and 'don't have time off for trade union activities'. Delegates opposing the amendment argued that postal ballots 'don't improve democracy' and that it was more important to address how to get people to meetings since attendance at Regional Council was the important factor in democracy. The motion to use a postal ballot for Regional Committee seats was lost. Approximately one-third of the Regional Council were for the motion, and two-thirds were against, which probably equated to a health service – local government split.

Concerns that the representation and participation of manual and health service workers was being limited were raised by a significant number of members. They found expression in a very explicit composite motion to the 1994 Conference:

This first UNISON Conference recognises that Fair Representation provided for under Rule has not been achieved in large parts of the structure. Manual workers, health workers and part-time women workers are badly under-represented. UNISON will fail to deliver if it is perceived to be and becomes a union dominated by white-collar members from local government. (UNISON, 1994e)

The motion, carried by Conference, instructed the NEC to:

1. Re-examine structures, particularly in the Regions and act wherever necessary to bring about fair representation;
2. Monitor the progress achieved continuously;
3. Report to the 1995 Conference with full details of the problems and proposals include any necessary rule changes.

Since a Joint Working Group had already been established to look into the fair representation of members within the union, it was decided that its work should continue and that its report should provide the basis for the NEC response to this motion. A very strong theme of the Working Group Report (UNISON, 1995a) related to the balance of power between members of the former partner unions.

Reconceptualising fair representation: former partner unions

The Working Group set out to collect information about the participation and involvement of members with particular reference to

- members from each of the three former partner unions;
- members from the various Service Groups and occupations;
- women;
- black members, disabled members and lesbian and gay members;
- part-time and low-paid workers and management grades.

The Working Group collected material using observation, reports from participants and paid officers, record keeping of participation and contribution to meetings and debates, questionnaires and surveys, interviews, focus groups and discussion and the analysis of documents. The report of the UNISON Joint Working Group (1995a) suggests that the feelings conveyed in my interviews were not uncommon. The following extracts are taken from the Report of the Joint Working Group and pertain to three focus groups established from delegates approached at random during one day of the 1994 Health Care Service Group Conference:

> Integration at branch level: Amongst the three groups where this was discussed so far there was very little evidence of any integration at branch level. There was some joint working, but it was felt there was a very low degree of trust, especially between ex-NALGO and the other two former partner unions at branch level. Ex-NUPE members were particularly suspicious and felt that they had to hang on to some separate branch arrangements at least for the time being to ensure some kind of representation for themselves and for their own ex-members.

> Regional Council and Committee: Most criticism and bitterness was levelled at the experience of Regional Councils and Regional Committees, especially by ex-NUPE and ex-COHSE. Members from these two former partner unions felt that they had been excluded by ex-NALGO by a combination of organisation, campaigning, the management of a 'slate' and an apparent sheer unwillingness on ex-NALGO's part to consider the importance of fair representation and proportionality and of making space for their sometimes rather less confident new colleagues from the other two partner unions. (UNISON, 1995a, p. 34)

This material was complemented by questionnaires completed by Regional Secretaries and other officers that indicated that Regional Council attendance from delegates 'from old COHSE and, especially, from old NUPE' was well below what might have been anticipated from membership figures. The returns also indicated that delegates from old NALGO took a bigger part in debate and were elected in larger numbers than 'would appear to have constituted reasonably proportional or fair representation'.

The Report concluded that the omission of specific provision for, or recognition of, the former partner unions in the merger negotiations was 'a laudable objective, even if arguably, and with the benefit of hindsight, rather naïve'. Such was the strength of feeling that former partner unions were not being fairly represented that the Working Group recommended that former union partner status should be monitored for the next two years after which it recommended monitoring by occupation. Although noted, less prominence was given to fair representation of black members and nothing was noted about the participation and integration of lesbian and gay members and disabled members. The next section discusses the manner in which preoccupations with gender and class tended to squeeze race out of the fair representation debate.

Fair representation and race

Although the definition of fair representation includes race, the first rule book included no electoral mechanism (such as the reservation of seats for black members) to guarantee this. Membership surveys suggest that approximately 10 per cent of UNISON members are black (Southern and Eastern Regional TUC Women's Rights Committee, 2000). Given that the low-paid seats were initially attached to annual salary, rather than an hourly rate, and black women tend to work full-time, low-paid seats were not likely to provide them with specific representative opportunities. The correlation between the lack of reserved seats for black members and the lack of black members on the first NEC and Local Government and Health Care SGEs is difficult to prove, but certainly there were no mechanisms that might push or pull black members into representative positions so as to mirror their membership of the union. Moreover, the pursuit of fair representation through low-paid seats distracted attention from diversity in relation to race, sexuality and disability. A member of the national LGSGE illustrated this most vividly with his comment that 'we have achieved fair representation here [on the LGSGE]'. This was said despite the absence of black members on the first LGSGE. From his perspective, fair representation referred to the balance between manual and non-manual workers.

Although the participation and involvement of black members, disabled members and lesbian and gay members was noted as an original term of reference for the Joint Working Group on participation and integration, little was said about this in the final report. It is not possible to know from the Report whether this reflects a wish not to ask about sensitive issues, or reflects a limited conception of fair representation. The Report notes the need for sensitivity when monitoring representation 'where matters of sexuality and disability were concerned and where self-identification and advocacy are matters primarily for the members themselves', but does not indicate the extent to which this concern limited their own research.

A motion amendment attempted to expand the remit of the NEC report on fair representation. The amendment sought to change motion 156 (noted above) to:

> Manual workers, health workers, *black, disabled and lesbian and gay members* and part-time women workers are badly under-represented. UNISON will fail to deliver if it is perceived to be and becomes a union dominated by *white, able bodied, heterosexual* white-collar members from local government. (UNISON, 1994e, added emphasis)

The amendment also instructed the NEC to provide representation for self-organised groups on the NEC. However, the Trade Union Act 1984 requires members of national executive committees to be directly elected by a postal ballot of all members. This means that all members must be elected to the committee, they cannot be co-opted onto the committee. The NEC opposed this amendment and Conference agreed with their decision and voted against it. As a consequence, the composite motion that was passed on fair representation did not include reference to black, disabled and lesbian and gay members.

Harlow, Hearn and Parkin (1995) use the words 'silence' and 'din' to describe and analyse domination and subordination in organisations. These terms are useful to describe the discussion of race within the Report of the Working Group. The Report summarises its findings in six categories: NEC, NDC, Activists Survey, first Service Group Elections (1994), Health Care Conference Focus Group Discussions, and regional level participation. There is a significance silence about the representation of black members in all six categories. The Report notes that black members are not fully represented on the NEC, that there is less progress on equal opportunities for black members but that this is now beginning, and that there is a serious risk of under-representation of black members. These references, however, are minor when compared with the 'din' of discussion about differences based on occupation, gender and former partner union. As the following example shows, a preoccupation with the representation of women and workers from across manual and white-collar grades can exclude representation across race.

Implementing fair representation at branch level

A merging Local Government branch was keen to ensure a fair balance between men and women and between APT&C and manual members. To this end the constitution set down three principles:

- that the branch secretary and the chair would not be members of the same sector, that is, if the secretary were an APT&C worker, the chair would be a manual worker;
- that at least two of the following posts (Health & Safety Officer, Equality Officer, Treasurer, Education Officer, and Welfare and Membership) would be taken by an APT&C worker and at least two would be taken by a manual worker;
- that at least 50 per cent of branch officers would be women.

Although these principles were trying to deal with representation across gender and class, they did not deal with the need to achieve representation across black and white members. This was particularly important, as approximately 50 per cent of branch members were black workers. The constitution came under pressure when the combination of candidates for uncontested and contested seats made it unlikely that the second and third set of principles would be met. In order to meet the principles of 50:50 male/female and 50:50 APT&C/manual, the branch automatically elected four candidates for the five identified seats – the other seat being uncontested. Those candidates who were not automatically elected were effectively selected out of the elections. This action was justified by noting that any other result would have been against proportionality and fair representation as it was defined between men/ women and APT&C/manual grades. Of these five seats, women occupied three, manual workers occupied two and black members occupied two. Thus, for these five seats, it would appear that proportionality and fair representation (across gender, class and race) had been achieved.

However, although these were the key officer posts, they were not the only seats on the committee and the combination of branch elections, and workgroup elections did not produce a committee that reflected the 50:50 balance between the black and white members. In addition, this process of automatic election led to a black male APT&C member being 'selected out' of the elections because his election would have resulted in a disproportionate number of white-collar members on the committee. The Black Workers Group in this branch was extremely unhappy with this outcome and made an official complaint to the Regional Committee alleging that the elections were discriminatory and demanding an investigation and re-election. The issue was eventually resolved and the complaint formally withdrawn when the elections were re-run with the active involvement of the Black Workers Group.

This vignette provides a number of insights into the implementation of proportionality and fair representation. It illustrates the manner in which a preoccupation with gender and class-based fair representation can squeeze out considerations of race-based representation. It also raises the practical implications of implementing a broader conception of fair representation. The following discussion illustrates how these two issues can be reconciled on a larger committee. The implication of ensuring the representativeness of a relatively small committee of directly elected members is discussed later.

Representative seats for black members on the NEC

A number of motion amendments for the first (1994) National Delegate Conference (NDC) called for the representation of black members and self-organised groups on the NEC. However, as noted above, NEC members must be directly elected and cannot be co-opted onto the committee. The NEC therefore opposed all such amendments. Conference agreed with this approach and no such amendments were passed. In 1995, the National Black Members Conference put forward a motion that noted the lack of adequate black representation on the UNISON National Executive Council and called for procedures to enable self-organised groups to have direct representation on the NEC (UNISON, 1995c). This became part of a composite motion and was the subject of much lobbying during the NDC to ensure that it was heard during Conference business. The composite was originally opposed by the NEC but was formally moved without debate on condition that the NEC would consider it post-NDC. This was a compromise position as had it been heard, opposed and lost, there would have been no obligation for the NEC to consider it post-NDC.

The Development and Organisation Committee of the NEC took responsibility for addressing the motion, working with the National Self-organised Committees and National Self-organised Liaison Group. As a consequence the rules were amended to provide for four additional seats – one men's seat, two women's seats and one low-paid women's seat (UNISON, 2000). Candidates are elected by the national constituency of UNISON, but must be nominated by at least 2 branches or regional self-organised groups. Although race is not specified as a criterion, the ability of regional self-organised groups to nominate candidates is expected to facilitate the election of black members (Labour Research, 2000).

Implementing fair representation in small committees

The NEC and the larger service group executives each consist of over 50 members. This large number allows a number of directly elected seats to be reserved for women without eliminating open competition for a significant number of non-reserved seats. At regional level, there were eight non-reserved seats on the Regional Committee. In branches, the total number of directly elected seats – with or without reservation – will be below ten. As the local government branch elections showed, it is extremely difficult to achieve fair representation across gender, class and race in very small numbers. As this study shows, it requires collective commitment to a shared concept of fair representation. It also requires greater participation by all membership groups.

A diverse candidature across all committee seats requires levels of participation from considerable numbers of members. The greater the diversity of members standing for election, the more chance of achieving diversity in representation. Reference has already been made to branch activists 'looking for women', and 'everyone having a hole for a low-paid woman on their slate'. Whilst some commentators might dislike what they see as a bureaucratic way of increasing representation from different groups, the rule-book commitments do seem to provide a legitimate route through which members can push themselves, or be pulled, into representative positions. Whilst the attempt to implement proportionality and fair representation created much bad feeling in the Local Government branch noted above, it did encourage a lot of black members (particularly young women) to become shop stewards and become actively involved in the union. It also prompted a white male manual worker to encourage a black female manual worker to stand with him on a job-share ticket for the post of branch secretary.

As noted in Chapter 3 above, the sharing of all branch posts is permitted in the rule book. A motion submitted to the 1996 National Delegate Conference provides an illustration of its potential:

> Our experience, as a branch, has shown that the single most effective method of encouraging and enabling women to become more active is to open all union positions to job-share. We have job-share officers (including the branch secretary) and job-share stewards and health and safety representatives (and since the inception of UNISON our conference delegation has always been at least proportional). We actively encourage everyone to consider sharing all their union activities. This has enabled our branch to achieve proportionality (or very close to it) through its structure. Within the East Midlands Region we also have all positions and committee memberships open to job-sharing – and this concept is enshrined within the rules. Here we also have encouraged more women to become involved (particularly within the women's committee, where all members automatically job-share). It makes sense to now share this achievement with other branches, regions and UNISON as a whole. Proportionality will not be achieved 'as if by magic' just because the rule book says so – we have to work at it. Here is something both positive and easy which we can use to achieve our goal. (UNISON, 1996a)

After this preamble, the motion instructed the NEC to encourage and facilitate job sharing of all UNISON positions 'from General Secretary down'. Despite the potential of this motion to significantly contribute to the debate about increasing members' activity within the union, the motion was not prioritised by sufficient parties and went unheard at the 1996 National Delegate Conference. However, job-sharing is a significant part of the UNISON Guidelines on Fair Representation published a year later (UNISON, 1997b). Indeed, job-sharing appears to be the preferred mechanism for increasing representation by individuals of oppressed social groups at a local level. A substantial part of the booklet relates to the implementation of fair representation at branch level. Branches are encouraged to undertake a branch audit of members, identify groups that are under-represented and draw up development plans to achieve 'improvement over the following years'. However, although branches are to develop ways of working that will encourage participation and activity, it is only job-sharing that is mentioned as a means of increasing representation of under-represented groups. There is no suggestion, or indication, that reserved seats could be used to address under-representation. The implication of this within UNISON as a whole is that it is appropriate to reserve seats at national and regional level but not at branch level. Whilst the majority of members may well accept the latter decision, not everyone is happy with the first.

Fair representation: bureaucratic exercise or a necessary element of democracy?

Some might argue that trying to achieve a representative balance between nine categories of difference that are not mutually exclusive and are not placed in any hierarchy was always an impossible task for UNISON to achieve. The implementation of proportionality has been facilitated by the ability to identify two mutually exclusive categories of membership (men and women) for the purposes of elections. One of the main consequences of fair representation being so wide-ranging is that it has provided a source of authority for a number of groups. As we have seen, this has resulted in conflict between different groups in the union. Manual women workers were concerned that proportionality was dealing with women's representation at the expense of class-based representation. Black workers were concerned that proportionality and fair representation across manual and white-collar workers were being achieved at the expense of a balance across black and white members. This conflict is vividly captured by these two motions put to the third (1996) National Delegate Conference. Two unmerged branches based in the same city submitted the motions:

> Conference welcomes the 'From Vision to Practice' report [Joint Working Group Report noted above] for its honesty and constructive approach. Conference recognises the danger of branches and regions paying lip-service to proportionality and fair representation whilst ensuring that effective power is wielded by an elite of highly paid, male, white-collar, local government workers. Conference assures that manual, health, other service groups and self-organised groups that the present trend will be immediately reversed. The promise that UNISON gave to women and low paid workers in particular must be delivered. It is intolerable that in any branch or region such members face repeated intimidation from men desperate to maintain a 'privileged' position within the union. Conference agrees that such reported instances be severely dealt with and, under rule, where investigated and proved. No. 2 branch. (UNISON, 1996a)

Amendment 162.1: Delete second paragraph and insert: Conference recognises the obstacles to achieving fair representation and proportionality, principally the lack of accurate membership information from many branches. Conference also notes that the UMS records are also woefully inadequate in terms of accurate membership information. Conference recognises the dangers of branches and regions becoming obsessed with the minutiae of definitions of fair representation and proportionality, sometimes to the exclusion of dealing with members' problems and conditions of service. Regional meetings have been bogged down with complex voting procedures. Whilst taking account of fair representation and proportionality, UNISON needs to re-affirm that our number one function is to provide the best possible services to all our members.

Conference notes that some factions within the union are now using this issue for their own short-term political interests and attempting to cause chaos within UNISON. Conference should re-affirm the principles of fair representation and proportionality as laudable goals but should note that to make the issue too prescriptive will be pure tokenism of the worst kind. UNISON should continue to appoint and elect people on the basis of merit and ability, taking into account fair representation and proportionality, not the other way round. No. 1 branch. (UNISON, 1996a)

As noted earlier, the concerns raised by these two branches are not unique. The fear expressed by the No. 1 branch that the implementation of proportionality and fair representation was affecting union effectiveness was raised in an article in *Socialist Appeal*. A branch secretary of a Local Government UNISON branch wrote it in a personal capacity

> Proportionality has meant that the energy of a branch can be dissipated in internal wrangling as different groups vye [*sic*] for positions. The fight against management can become less important than the fight against each other. No wonder the union officials appreciate the value of reserved seats! (Short, 1995)

This article also articulates another concern raised by the No. 1 branch – that elections should be on the basis of merit and ability. This branch secretary argues that 'quotas may mean incompetent or self serving members get on a branch committee and be impossible to dislodge through election.' The *Socialist Appeal* article was reproduced in the branch newsletter of another Local Government branch with the following introduction:

On the incoming NEC there are 13 reserved seats for low paid women ... Of these seats one was contended, 8 elected unopposed and 4 received no nominations. Only 5 other seats were uncontended, most of these in the Service Groups. It therefore pays in UNISON terms to be a low paid woman if you want to become a career bureaucrat. I hope the article opposite stimulates a response, either agreement or opposition.

These arguments are informed by an overwhelming concern that, given the opportunity, officers will use power against members. From this perspective, in the *Socialist Appeal* article, the branch secretary argues that proportionality and fair representation have been used as a 'radical' cover for the union's 'lack of activity over government attacks on public spending which disproportionately affect women employees'. Her argument that it has been used as a 'recipe for divide and rule' is an important discussion point. As noted above, the implementation of fair representation has highlighted divisions between manual and white-collar workers, between former NUPE and former NALGO members, and between black and white members. However, does this conflict necessarily mean that fair representation should not be attempted?

Phillips (1993) argues that politics based on identity (rather than interests) are far more likely to encourage fragmentation or mutual hostility between groups. Some might use such arguments to explain – and argue against – the intensity of lobbying for increased representation by manual workers and black members. However, as noted by Young (1990), unless confronted with different perspectives on social relations and events, different values and language, most people tend to assert their perspective as universal. Could it be that it is privileged groups (in this case, white members) who are identifying themselves in opposition to oppressed groups and that it is *their* denial and resistance that is a root cause of the conflict?

Although very painful for the combatants, the fiercely contested concept of fair representation is arguably the first test of democracy within UNISON. Using the phrases of Harlow et al. (1995), if manual workers had remained silent and not created a 'din', fair representation could have been limited to part-time manual women workers. If black activists had remained silent, fair representation could have been limited to a class-based interpretation. Some of the rules of the game have been changed to support members of oppressed social groups. Regional self-organised groups can now nominate candidates for four additional seats on the NEC. As noted in Chapter 3, seats are now reserved for self-organised groups at national service group conferences. The rules related to the low-paid women's seats were amended at the 1997 Conference. They changed the salary-based criterion to an hourly rate. The low-paid women's seats are now reserved for female members earning less than a basic hourly rate of £4.80, (this amount to be uprated annually by the increase in median earnings, as defined by the New Earnings Survey in the October immediately preceding the election (UNISON, 1997a). However, the shaping of fair representation is not the only test of democracy, and as argued in the *Socialist Appeal* article above, an important second test relates to the policy outcomes of the union – issues discussed in Chapters 8 and 9.

Summary and discussion

Chapters 4 and 5 illustrated how proportionality has provided women with immediate and unequivocal access to decision-making arenas. The chapters also showed how the implementation of proportionality through multi-representative seats enabled privileged groups to take advantage of the consequent increases in lay representation. In the main, the chapters indicated that it was paid officers, rather than men as a group, who were likely to resist the implementation of proportionality. This chapter has noted a different set of processes surrounding the shaping of fair representation.

First, the definition of fair representation itself frustrates the achievement of unequivocal access to decision making. Nine potentially overlapping categories are identified in fair representation. Should this definition be changed? The Joint Working Group on Fair Representation concluded

> It is clear that the definition of fair representation, as it currently stands in the Rule Book, constitutes an excellent set of principles but is a poor and too general guide to put into practice. Indeed, to some, it appears so difficult fully to comply with, that they shy away from it altogether as setting impracticable demands. (UNISON, 1995a, p. 42)

The attempt to encapsulate the key dimensions of membership has provided scope for different parties to use it as justification for their representation. Pre-merger discussions decided that emphasis should be placed on low-paid women. Considerable effort, post-merger, has been directed at shaping fair representation so that it relates to the balance of manual and non-manual workers. As noted, this has sometimes taken precedence over the fair representation of black and white members. This raises questions about the definition of privileged groups within UNISON.

Young (1990) notes that for every oppressed group, there is a group that is privileged in relation to that group. So far, men have been identified as a privileged group in relation to the oppressed social group of women. This discussion of fair representation has identified two more privileged groups. Working-class members and black members are identified as an oppressed social group. Each group has been subject to at least one, if not more, of the following sites of oppression: exploitation, marginalisation, powerlessness, cultural imperialism and violence. Thus, middle-class and white members could be identified as privileged groups. Young admits that group differences cut across one another and are multiple, fluid and shifting. This makes it difficult to accurately identify sites of resistance and oppression. Are the former NUPE members fighting for representation because they are members of an oppressed group within the new union, or because they are members of a former privileged group of men that is losing power? Does opposition to the full implementation of fair representation derive from concerns about operational practicalities or does it derive from an appreciation that diversity will require a fairer share of a finite number of seats? Chapters 4 and 5 showed how multi-representative seats enabled those already favoured with power to retain representative seats. Adding more dimensions of diversity requires a rebalancing of representation that cannot be achieved through adding extra seats. Hyman argues that solidarity between different groupings within unions presupposes 'a process of internal education and argument of major extent and intensity' (1989, p. 185). The role of self-organised groups in UNISON has been part of that argument.

7 The Role of Women's Self-Organisation

This book is examining the extent to which UNISON is pursuing a different type of democracy – a democracy that attempts the equalisation of power between oppressed social groups and privileged groups. So far, the book has shown how UNISON has provided rights of representation for individual members of oppressed social groups. Chapters 4 and 5 have shown how proportionality can generate new sources of authority for individual women. Chapter 6 has shown how fair representation can generate new sources of authority for black members. As noted in Chapter 2, generating new sources of authority for individual members of an oppressed social group is not the same as generating them for oppressed social groups. This chapter deals with the manner in which UNISON's rule book generates new sources of power for oppressed social groups.

Chapter 2 made a distinction between self-organisation and group representation, noting that the former provided space for oppressed groups to develop their collective ideas and the latter provided representative routes to partial or full participation in decision making. Chapter 3 indicated that UNISON's rule book provides support for self-organised groups and limited forms of group representation for self-organised groups. Group representation was limited by its location and by its lack of coercive power. Thus within UNISON's rule book, self-organisation is the primary means of equalising power between privileged and oppressed social group.

The preceding chapters have illustrated how privileged and oppressed social groups within UNISON have shaped the concepts of proportionality and fair representation. The interpretation and implementation of self-organisation and group representation is no less contested. This chapter shows how the rule book has provided obstacles and opportunities for those making and shaping the rules on self-organisation and group representation. Material was collected from the structures and elections of women's self-organised groups in two regions, denoted here (though not by UNISON) as Region 1 and Region 2 and the National Women's Committee. I attended meetings, conferences and educational activities related to each structure, interviewed activists and officers associated with each committee/group. I collected additional data through a questionnaire administered at two women-only activities and the reading of union documents.

Young stresses the need for the self-organisation of group members 'so that they achieve collective empowerment and a reflective understanding of their collective experience and interests in the context of the society' (1990, p. 184). As noted in Chapter 3, the rule book provides self-organised groups with resources and decision-making powers – both aspects associated with supporting the autonomy of self-organised groups (Briskin, 1999). A third element that supports autonomy is an organised and politicised constituency. This chapter identifies two approaches that women have taken to self-organsation. Each approach targets a different constituency of women, which in turn, has implications for the institutional practices adopted in each regional group.

The first approach is seen most clearly in Region 1. It combines informal constituency building amongst all women with the use and extension of formal rights to group representation. This approach could be categorised as the generation of authority and influence through self-organisation and group representation. A key element of this approach is to do things differently and adopt new institutional practices within the self-organised group.

The second approach was found in Region 2 and emanates from a different interpretation of women's position in UNISON. This seeks the equalisation of power through constituency building amongst women activists and their active involvement in mainstream activities. This could be categorised as the generation of authority and influence through women's organisation. This has required a change to the rules for self-organisation. The two approaches to self-organisation find expression in debates about the constituency and activity of the National Women's Conference. The chapter concludes that there are important distinctions to be made between women's self-organisation and women's organisation which have implications for the representation of women as an oppressed social group.

Self-organisation in Region 1

Open access to all women

The aim of self-organisation in Region 1 was to encourage *all* women to come forward and participate in regional women's events and education with the express intention that the work of self-organisation should be focused on the concerns and needs of women. To this end, the women's structure in this region was based on two elements: a Regional Women's Forum, and Regional Women's Co-ordinating Team. The next sections examine these two structures and illustrate how they provide a different set of institutional practices within UNISON. The chapter then discusses the institutional practices emanating from these structures.

The Women's Co-ordinating Team   Like the Regional Council, the Regional Women's Forum is responsible for electing members to a 'management committee' at its Annual General Meeting. The women's self-organised group in Region 1 decided to call their management committee the 'Women's Co-ordinating Team'. The rule book prescribes that such committees should consist of 'representatives of each relevant group at branch level'. The word 'representatives' implies that women would require nomination from their branches to the Women's Co-ordinating Team. The interim Women's Group saw this requirement as providing a potential block to women's participation – particularly, where there was a lack of communication within the branch.

To reconcile their wishes with those of the rule book, they proposed that the elections for the Women's Co-ordinating Team should consist of volunteers as well as branch nominees and that the volunteers/nominees should stand for election to service group seats. Thus women in a Local Government branch might be nominated or volunteer for Local Government Service Group (LGSG) seats. The Co-ordinating Team saw this as a means of widening the 'net that women came from'. The potential for candidates to volunteer for a position on the Co-ordinating Team contrasts with the mainstream equivalent. Candidates for the Regional Committee can only stand for election if nominated by a branch. When questioned about the accountability of these service group representatives (by a member at the 1994 Regional Forum), the Women's Co-ordinating Team said that women would not be representatives of the service groups, but would be 'representative women'.

The Regional Women's Forum This Forum is intended to be a large body of members (approximately 150 women) who determine priorities and policies for the region, and in this respect it is similar to the mainstream Regional Council. However, one fundamental difference occurs which reflects the desire to support the inclusivity of women's organisation. The Forum is open to any women. Women may attend because they wish to or because they have been nominated by their branch to attend. This is different to the mainstream Regional Council, to which attendance is only achievable through branch nomination.

The first Regional Women's Forum attracted a lot of interest and 97 women registered to attend the Forum in 1994. Of the 60 who attended on the day, 55 per cent completed an attendance form. In the main, they indicate that a relatively wide range of women attended the Forum. Twenty-four per cent of respondents had manual jobs, 33 per cent had clerical/admin. jobs and 33 per cent had professional jobs. Thirty per cent of respondents worked part-time. Of those responding, only one could be defined as 'low paid' according to UNISON's criterion, which in 1994 was defined as earning up to and including £5,000 per year, but 21 per cent of respondents earned less than £7,000, and a further 15 per cent earned less than £10,000. Respondents were given the opportunity to self-identify themselves in relation to race, sexuality and disability. Of the 33 respondents, five women self-identified themselves as black, one as Asian, two as disabled and five as out-lesbians. In view of the decision to encourage all women to attend regardless of their activity within the union, it is interesting to note that 20 per cent said they were inactive in the branch.

Focusing on the needs and concerns of women

Women's newsletter   The women's newsletter provides another opportunity for women to 'access' women's self-organisation in Region 1. The newsletter is produced four times a year and, at the time of my research, the print-run was 7500. Copies are bulk mailed to branches, with a sizeable number (approximately 500) also being direct mailed to individual women.   The newsletter is seen as one way of getting information about women's events and women's concerns past 'gatekeepers' at branch level. It provides a unique way of including women in debates, focuses on issues concerning women and allows direct advertisement of such events as the National Women's Conference, and Regional Women's meetings, which women might not otherwise receive.

The response to the distribution of the newsletter within the region is interesting to note, and led the Chair of the Team to reflect that the women had almost become victims of their own success. Originally monies for the newsletter came from the regional publicity budget, but a decision had been made that the newsletter had to be resourced from the women's budget. In addition, some people were having thoughts about having a regional newsletter (distribution three times each year), with a one-to-four page insert for women. The Co-ordinating Team felt they should fight for the continuation of a separate newsletter, and a member of the Team pursued this point in the Regional Committee in her capacity as a member of the Regional Committee Publicity Sub-committee. Prior to the matter being raised at Regional Committee, women organised around the issue and were able to mobilise bias and votes in favour of continued regional funding of the women's newsletter.

This was a positive outcome for the women's self-organisation in this region. The newsletter represents a different way of communicating with members and specifically highlights women's issues. The Women's Officer in Region 1 wanted her article on women and Compulsory Competitive Tendering to make women in white-collar jobs realise that it could be them next. Other Women's Officers contrasted such newsletters with general material being distributed within the union to members that was called 'dry' and 'inaccessible'. They argued that union material should be more feminist and should make women angry. If this newsletter had become a supplement in a general regional newsletter, the women might have lost the control they had over distribution; just as important, they may have lost the ability to write copy that 'made women angry'.

A separate space for all women

Like the Regional Council, the Regional Women's Forum plans to meet four times a year, but in contrast, whilst all Council meetings are to the same format, it is proposed that one forum is a motion-based meeting, and the others will be a mixture of styles (including workshop-based meetings). In an effort to move the venue around the region, the 1994 and 1995 Forum were in different geographical locations. The constitution notes that the Forum should include opportunities to:

- share and exchange information;
- develop skills;
- set the agenda for women's self-organisation;
- influence the work of service conditions and other regional committees;
- influence the work of the National Women's Committee;
- to enable women to network and integrate experienced and new members;
- *and* should include a social or fun element. It is possible to enjoy trade union activity! (original emphasis)

One of the stated aims of the group was to 'create an open and supportive environment, without discrimination or intimidation, that is a comfortable atmosphere in which women can develop and learn'. A letter to delegates attending the first Forum illustrates this intention:

> There will be an opportunity to ask questions at the event but some women may feel nervous about doing so in front of a large group and would rather have someone put questions on their behalf. I have provided a form on which you can write your questions or put your point, proposal.

This provision goes against the norm of earning the right to say something through standing up in front of people and this facility was used by a few women at the Forum. One member used the facility to formally propose a motion rather than standing up and presenting it in front of the 60 attendees of the Forum. I investigated women's views of the Forum and their feelings about the discussion of the proposals for self-organisation that was intended to be relaxed and open. None of the 16 women who responded to my questionnaire found the atmosphere discouraged them from taking part in the debate. Thirteen of the women found it interesting and eight agreed that it had helped them understand more about self-organisation, and more about the way unions debate issues. A number of questionnaire respondents made these additional comments:

> Although I didn't stand up and speak I would have liked to take a more active part – NERVES!

> It made me feel like getting up to speak (maybe next time I'll have the courage).

The atmosphere was very comfortable and people were approachable.

Everyone was friendly, when talking to others they listen to what you have to say.

Given me confidence being amongst women who had also suffered male oppression during their lives.

Betty's experience illustrated the inclusivity of women's organisation in this region. Betty's interest in the Forum had arisen from her contact with the Women's Officer on a women-only course and had been underpinned by references in the women's newsletter. It had not derived from any activity at her branch. She was under the impression that there was nothing to do at her own workplace due to the existence of a shop steward within her department. Indeed, she noted that she only gets involved in the branch when the shop steward is ill. Betty nominated herself for a position on the Regional Co-ordinating Team but felt moved to withdraw her nomination at the Regional Forum, noting

Other nominees have lots of experience. Experience discriminates and I feel that I could not compete. I would therefore like to withdraw my nomination.

After Betty offered her resignation, there were many expressions of support from Forum attendees and members of the Women's Co-ordinating Team. A number of members asked her not to stand down, saying that it was important for non-experienced women to come forward. A year later Betty stood for a seat on the National Women's Committee. Her election text read

I am Betty. I am a 35 year old black woman. I have been on the Regional Women's Co-ordinating Team for about a year. At first I was very reluctant, but with the help and support from the other members, I now feel very confident. With the knowledge I have gained I would like to be given a chance to take some of what I have learned to the National Women's Committee.

The Regional Women's Forum was described as a 'women only event organised by women for women' and provided opportunities for women to participate in a number of workshops. Topics at the 1994 and 1995 Forum were pensions, domestic violence, self-organisation, sexual harassment, tackling work-related stress, personal development, women's health at work, selling yourself at interview, and discrimination at work. Participants responding to a questionnaire indicated that the workshops were the most useful aspect of the day and noted that these topics were not regularly discussed in their own branches. A few illustrations of these workshops are provided below.

Domestic violence workshop   Women attending this workshop felt very strongly that domestic violence should be a trade union issue and made a number of recommendations which showed their desire to make connections between the private and public sphere. During my research, a Women's Committee in another UNISON Region produced a twelve-page A5 booklet entitled 'Violence in the Home'. The Co-ordinating Team purchased 700 copies for distribution within Region 1.

Pensions workshop   This workshop was available at both the 1994 and 1995 Forums, and the facilitator noted that the main concern amongst women taking part was a lack of understandable information, both for their own personal needs and for dissemination to the members who approached them with queries. Four major issues were highlighted as important to women within UNISON: discrimination in pension schemes; equalisation of state pension age, privatisation and pensions, and legal protection of pensions.

Discrimination at work workshop   This workshop enabled the particular concerns of black women to be raised. The women discussed different forms of discrimination and talked about how the union could help more. Suggestions from the attendees included:

- highlighting incidents of discrimination;
- taking people more seriously when they complain;
- ongoing education and awareness of discrimination for activists and officers;
- the union needing to be seen as trustworthy and confidential;
- more black representatives, otherwise there is a feeling of isolation.

Using group representation rights

The objectives of the women's self-organisation in Region 1 highlight the desire for women's self-organisation to influence the work of various mainstream Regional Committees, and 'get issues of concern to women onto the agenda at regional level'. The Regional Women's Co-ordinating Team worked with the other three self-organised groups to increase the number of representatives on the Regional Council and Committee from one to two. During my study of women's self-organisation in this region, I was able to observe a few examples of group representation at Regional Council and Regional Committee. Each example related to shaping the participation and representation of women members. Mainstream discussion of the women's newsletter has already been discussed. Concerns raised at Regional Committee about the constituency of National Women's Conference are discussed later. Another concern related to the payment of childcare expenses for conference attendance.

Although members with children had been provided with a crèche facility at the National Women's Conference, it had been provided at the exclusion of childcare expenses for those leaving their children at home. That is, the union provided one childcare support facility, rather than a range of options. A number of women argued that they did not want to 'drag their children up to conference' and that some schools did not approve of children missing school. Since it was not possible to claim childcare expenses for those left at home, one delegate had been unable to attend the Conference. Another women said that she had left her children with a friend, noting that single mothers do not have partners to look after the children at night. It was apparent at meetings I attended that considerable numbers of women felt 'let down' by the manner in which the union handled the whole issue of childcare needs. In response the women-only activists in Region 1 raised the issue of childcare needs at the mainstream Regional Committee and a letter expressing concern was sent from the mainstream Regional Committee to the national Finance Office.

Despite these examples, however, my attendance at the Women's Co-ordinating Team and a number of Regional Committee and Council meetings led me to suspect that few issues raised by the women were being aired in mainstream committees (bar those issues concerning self-organisation and childcare expenses). Towards the end of my research

Tina, a key activist, spoke about her expectations, and experience, of being a member of the Women's Co-ordinating Team:

> I thought they would develop a women's agenda within the region that they would pursue within the trade union structures, and take on things in support of women. I don't personally think we have been very successful ... I feel that no women's agenda has been developed.

Tina noted that the members of the Co-ordinating Team had been on a learning curve and needed time to develop and it is necessary to remember that at the time of my research the union was in the first throes of its new existence. However, I gained the impression from observations of the Team, regional committees, and a number of interviews, that the encouragement of new women within the region would not result in women's concerns being addressed in the mainstream, unless linkages were forged with women who were already active in the region. Tina said she did not believe there was any feeling of women's unity at regional level:

> Women operate as individuals. Quite a lot of women involved at high levels don't see the relevance of women's organisation or women's solidarity. These women follow a gender-blind agenda – the gender aspect being of secondary importance.

Branch activity

The Women's Officer wanted to focus the work of the Co-ordinating Team on branch activity, noting that 'branch based women are key to effective women's organisation'. In practice, there was no structure to facilitate this and women's self-organised activity relied heavily on the efforts of the Women's Officer and work by members of the Co-ordinating Team in their own branch. The Women's Officer gave an example of the difficulty of becoming personally involved in the setting-up of self-organised groups at branch level. An interested group of women had asked her to talk about setting up their own self-organised group. However, both the paid officer responsible for the branch and the branch secretary, were offended by what they saw as interference with their 'patch'. The branch secretary contacted the regional office to complain that the original approach to the Women's Officer, and her subsequent action, should have been directed through the 'official channels'. A more fruitful channel to organising women at branch level was through the regional LGSG.

The (female) Head of Local Government in Region 1 involved the Women's Officer in a number of issues. She had given her an open invitation to the Officers' meetings within the LGSG, and had asked her to run seminars for women on Equal Pay for Work of Equal Value, and Women and Compulsory Competitive Tendering (CCT). The Women's Officer commented that her close involvement with this service group would facilitate the inclusion of Branch Equality Officers in the seminars in CCT. The importance of their inclusion relates to the fact that key negotiators were always invited to such seminars, but Equality Officers were not, and their attendance might provide women wider access to CCT discussions than might otherwise have been the case. The Women's Officer had sent a memo to the Regional Management Team regarding the definition of her role, following which the Regional Secretary had written to all heads of service groups noting that they should involve her in their business. The Women's Officer compared the response she had received from the (female) Head of the Regional Local Government Group with the lack of interest shown by the (male) Head of the Regional Health Care Group.

The Women's Officer told me of a number of ways in which she had become involved in branch activity. In a County Council, she had pursued the possibility of a partnership between the employer (a Direct Service Organisation) and UNISON, whereby the employer would provide money for tutors and paid leave for the UNISON Return to Learn course. In another County Council, the Women's Officer had been involved in developing an action plan for fair representation and proportionality. On at least two occasions, she had become involved when members of the union had been harassed at work. Following one of the cases in a District Council, she had assisted in the development of a harassment policy and the proposed appointment of harassment advisors. In another Local Authority, a number of women had been traumatised by the activities of a manager who had been bullying and harassing them. Working with a member of the Co-ordinating Team, the Women's Officer had developed a Personal Development course and used it to rebuild women's confidence. The initiative had been jointly funded by the branch and employer and the member of the Co-ordinating Team concerned noted that it was 'ground-breaking stuff'. However, whilst this had obviously provided much needed support for the women, it had not been a means of increasing the number of women activists within the branch. The member involved noted that they were struggling to get self-organisation going in the branch and that it was only the same few women who attended the meetings. She herself had started a few initiatives with the Equal Opportunities officers, such as subscribing to *Everywoman*, and investigating the purchase of personal alarms for all members, but what she really wanted to see was a working committee. It is this notion of a 'working committee' at branch level that lies at the heart of the constitution in Region 2 – albeit targeted at a different constituency of women.

Women's organisation in Region 2

'It starts at the branch'

Region 1 did not want to prescribe women's involvement at the branch level, and members of the Regional Forum and Regional Co-ordinating Team did not have to be nominated by their branch. In contrast, the constitution of Region 2 targets women who are active at branch level. As a consequence, the aims and objectives of women's organisation in Region 2 differ considerably from those of Region 1. Region 2 does not mention 'self-organisation' in any part of their constitution. This omission is a deliberate strategy, as explained by the Women's Officer:

> The philosophy is different in this region. The Regional Women's Committee does not see self-organisation as useful. How helpful was self-organisation in NALGO? In this region, we don't use the terminology of self-organisation. We use the words of women's structure, women's committee, proportionality and fair representation. Too many women fall into the trap of self-organisation ... women's self-organisation has no power, its principles are not addressed in practice ... the other self-organised groups are different, but the rule book treats them the same. I have always argued that women's structure is different, the others are minorities, but since the majority of members are women, women are not the minority. Assertive women don't want to be seen as oppressed or as 'victims'. Women have the rules for proportionality, the other groups don't. Women have priority, women are different, but this is not clear at national level.

The next section examines the structures that support women who are already active in the union. The women's structure in this region is based on four elements: Branch Equality Officers (Women), Branch Women's Committees, Regional Women's Committee and Regional Women's Forum.

Branch level structures The Interim Women's Committee in Region 2 took advantage of the rule by which each branch committee is to include Equality Officer(s). Their proposed constitution invited branches to elect a Branch Equality Officer for Women (BEOW) under this rule. Whilst the tasks of this officer are defined in the Code of Good Branch Practice, it is the intention in Region 2 that the BEOW is a functional link between branches and the Regional Women's Committee. The BEOW was also to be the convenor of the Branch Women's Committee. The proposed constitution of the Branch Women's Committee also represents a significant difference to perceptions of women's self-organisation in Region 1. Whereas branches in Region 1 were encouraged to hold meetings for all women, Region 2 proposed that a Branch Women's Committee be established in each branch, which would be composed of women shop stewards, and would work to the following objectives:

- to support women activists;
- to build women's organisation – including assisting in the recruitment and support of new stewards;
- to monitor proportionality and fair representation;
- to contribute to the development of policy with regard to issues of particular concern to women.

The rule book allows for women's self-organised groups at branch level, and the Code of Good Branch Practice notes that 'each self-organised group must be accessible and open to all members' within that identified membership group. Since the Women's Branch Committee is to consist only of women shop stewards, this does not constitute a self-organised group. An interview with the Women's Officer revealed the philosophy underpinning this alternative structure. The Officer argued that, in her experience, manual and part-time women members do not attend women's committees, at which point self-organised groups become very unrepresentative. It was clear from the interview, that the Women's Officer believed that self-organised groups at branch level were not necessarily supportive or constructive for women's representation, and whilst they might raise feminist awareness, participants were not necessarily representative of women in work groups/branches, because of high non-attendance. The Women's Officer talked about her belief in an alternative strategy which encouraged women shop stewards to represent women members interests, to organise where necessary to support each other, and to organise campaigns. The Women's Officer argued that if they put into place a structure where women were allocated positions and responsibility, this would become a 'working forum'. She told me that the female Regional Convenor also believed that the women's structure should be a working structure 'delivering service to the membership'. In the Women's Officer's opinion, democracy was ensured through representation and accountability. She noted:

> The majority of regions are encouraging women who have nothing to do with their branch. Some people think the more the merrier, but someone pays – who pays? ... women have to run the union, so we need to teach and enable women to run it – making it possible for them to intervene. If there is no membership base and women are not shop stewards then we might be parachuting women members in at high levels. Whose interests do they represent?

Regional structures

Regional Women's Committee   The Co-ordinating Team in Region 1 consists of members occupying service-group seats, low-paid women's seats, women nominated from other self-organised groups and representatives of the Regional Committee. The service-group seats do not relate to specific branches. Women can volunteer for these seats and do not require prior nomination by their branches. Any contested elections are held at the Women's Forum. This contrasts with the constitution of the Women's Committee in Region 2.

First, women in Region 2 cannot volunteer themselves for election. They require nomination by their branch or regional service group. Secondly, representatives are to be directly elected from branches, as opposed to indirect elected from an intermediate body, such as the Forum in Region 1. Third, an attempt has been made to include representatives from most local government and health care branches in the region. Local Government and Health Authority districts have been grouped to provide 16 local government seats and nine health seats. The other service groups are eligible for one seat, to be indirectly elected through the appropriate regional service group. There is no provision for the election of low-paid seats as in Region 1, but women in low-paid seats on the NEC and the National Women's Committee are automatically members of the Committee. The use of the representative links between the Women's Committee and the Regional Council and Committee in Region 2 is discussed in Chapter 9.

The Women's Officer talked about the work of the Women's Committee:

> The priority of the Women's Committee is to organise and develop skills through education and training programmes. Most of the work is about organising shop stewards training for women who are shop stewards or interested in becoming stewards. We want change, we're not converting them into men ... we're organising women locally to be confident in the union. For example, delivering basic shop steward training courses where we can give a different view to the myth of what shop stewards are ... It's about giving them the confidence to do what they do instinctively, but to give them the support that is needed. It's about raising issues for women through educational trade union structures: women and pensions, women and state benefits, and representing women's issues at work – changing the agenda, for example, CCT – rights of part-time workers, women and pensions, equal part-time rights – not things men see as agenda. The view of the committee is that the agenda is from the top at the moment – but that it will come through.

Regional Forum The constitution allows for a Regional Women's Forum to be held at least once a year with specific objectives:

- to identify key areas of work for the Regional Women's Committee;
- to develop the role of Branch Equality Officers;
- to identify key areas of concern for women members in the Region;
- to develop work on women's organisation, representation and campaigns within branches.

In the words of the proposed constitution, the Forum is to be 'educational, informative and organisational'. There was no mention of 'fun' in this constitution. The Regional Forum was to be workshop based and accompanied by training sessions, to give women confidence, knowledge and skills to participate in the mainstream union structures. There was no mechanism for policy making at the meeting. In stark contrast to the inclusive Forum established in Region 1, the Forum is to consist of members of the Regional Women's Committee and Branch Equality Officers for Women. It is *not* open to all women within the region and there is only a guarantee that at least one Forum will be held each year in contrast to four proposed in Region 1.

The Chair of the Women's Committee justified the lack of policy-making processes at the Forum by noting the difficulty of getting fair representation at conferences, since they tended to eliminate shift workers, part-timers and women, who are predominantly carers. This part of the constitution was heavily criticised when presented at the mainstream Regional Committee for approval. One member noted that in his opinion:

> It is dangerous not to have significant part of the regional conference as motion based, since the women would only be discussing issues, they would not be able to make policy. There is a danger that it would turn into a non-policy body.

In responding, the Chair of the Women's Committee referred to past conferences where 60 women had registered, and only 45 had attended. She referred to feedback that indicated that women who were most adept at speaking ran motion-based conferences. She argued that some women feel more confident talking in a smaller workshop situation, than in a motion-based situation. The Chair repeated these comments in a later interview:

> I would like to have an all-women forum to which any woman could come but we would have to make sure that it was not railroaded by those women who are more articulate than the others. We don't want to replace one domination by another. We want a mix of ages and abilities – all trade unionists without any ulterior motives.

That the Forum in Region 1 is open to all women who are interested in attending was seen as a measure of its inclusiveness. At first sight, therefore, the Forum in Region 2 appears very exclusive. However, in other ways it could be seen as being more inclusive. If all branches have a Branch Equality Officer for Women and all such Officers are directly invited to the Forum, then this offers the opportunity for all branches to be represented at the Forum. In this way it promotes the inclusion of members in a more systematic manner than through open invitation. If effective, it could facilitate the participation of women from different occupations, different geographical locations and different former-partner unions. It does require women, however, to take a representative role at branch level. Commenting on the differences in the two constitutions, the Chair of the Women's Committee in Region 2 noted:

> Our constitution is based on the need for responsibility and accountability. ... Everything should start at the branch. You need involvement at the branch, education and training, and sympathetic environment ... the Branch Equality Officer only forum has to be in the structure, otherwise if it were a meeting for any women, it could get taken over by the 'conference cat'. A woman's first step would be all-women's education. Weekend women's schools are for any women, especially new women. Such weekends enable women to find out more. They stimulate interest.

Women-only shop steward education

The Women's Committee introduced a planned programme of training for women stewards which would comprise a series of courses launched with a 'women's weekend school'. It was intended that this programme would build up skills and confidence over the period of twelve months, with the ultimate aim to empower and encourage women to become more active in the main trade union structure and to encourage them to participate in the broader regional education programme. During and up to September 1995, the Women's Committee was responsible for organising six courses for women that attracted a total of 99 women members. The courses were:

- Speaking up and Being Heard;
- Negotiating on Women's Issues;
- Speaking in Public;
- Recruiting and Organising Women Members;
- Women's Weekend School;
- Induction Course.

I attended two courses, Recruiting and Organising Women Members, and Women's Weekend School. Both of these appeared to achieve the aims indicated by the Women's Officer, namely, 'organising women locally to be confident in the union' and 'delivering basic shop steward training courses where we can give a different view to the myth of what shop stewards are'. A high number of new shop stewards were attracted to the courses. The courses were organised around role-playing activities that enabled women to engage with, and articulate, the practicalities of workplace union activity. These activities enabled me to obtain information about women's concerns.

Women's concerns A number of the recruitment activities highlighted the importance of the union addressing the concerns of workers at the workplace, and course members discussed ways in which they could get a higher priority for issues affecting women. When asked to identify women's needs they noted the following:

- discriminatory impact of some sickness policies (that is, they don't take account of biological differences, such as women's periods);
- maternity/paternity leave;
- childcare facilities; policies to take account of children's illness;
- pension rights and pensionable age;
- promotion;
- impact of multi-skilling on women.

During a Women's Weekend course, small groups gave five-minute presentations to the rest of the course and brought many of their collective experiences to bear in their presentations. In contrast to much of the discussion at the weekend that had been about 'members', the topics focused attention on women's concerns. The group looking at Women's Health at Work recommended a breast cancer-screening scheme. The group looking at Equality for Women recommended action on job segregation, better care facilities, positive action training, and action on low pay. A third group looked at low pay and made recommendations for job evaluation, and the study of wage differentials. Other groups looked at the NHS pay campaign, low pay, proportionality and fair representation, and maternity and paternity rights, and the experiences of women at work came out very clearly in all of them. For a number of women, this was the first time that they had spoken in front of such a large group (approximately 25), so the exercise provided them with the experience of talking to others, making recommendations, and answering questions. At the end of the weekend, course members were encouraged to identify a few key things to do in the next few months: 'to increase women's involvement in the union and raise issues of importance to women with members, the union and employers'. Of those volunteering to talk about their personal action plans, women identified the following:

- workplace nursery;
- proportionality/fair representation: of thirty stewards, five are women;
- more meetings/more members;
- branch officers support;
- discuss contracts of part-time workers with management;
- ex-members – encourage to rejoin;
- discuss better pay and conditions;
- build in proportionality in merged branch;
- education;
- reinforce image of union.

The weekend appeared to be extremely successful in educating newly active women in a supportive environment. The residential nature of the course, together with the use of group work, enabled a number of women to network across the region, and although there were some points of tension during the weekend, women felt it was possible to express their views and opinions in an open manner. However, it is important to note that concentrating on the education of women who are already active within the union is very different to the approach of other women's self-organised groups. Reproduced below is an extract from a letter sent from a Regional Women's Committee, in another region, to their Regional Council:

> A commitment of becoming an 'activist' however should not be a condition of attending such a course, and this had never been the intention of the Region.

> The X Region's Education Policy and Statement on Women's Education states that:

> 'Educational activity should help to encourage women to think about progressing from inactive member to active member, to activist, to "leader".

> However, there should be no assumption that becoming an active member must lead to becoming an activist; or that becoming an activist necessarily involves becoming a leader ...'

> This meeting therefore urges branches to encourage women's attendance on education courses and to be mindful of the fact that while members may be more inclined to give a commitment to union activities after attending a course, a prior commitment shall not be required by the branch as a condition of the member's attendance on the course.

Changing the rules of self-organisation

The rule-book commitments to self-organisation enabled the women in Region 1 to change institutional practices within their self-organised groups, without challenging the rules. In contrast, the women in Region 2 were not able to adopt the institutional norm of branch-based accountability without an adaptation of the rule book. Thus Region 1's strategy of doing things differently was not challenged by the mainstream but Region 2's strategy of doing the same as the mainstream brought them into direct conflict with members of the mainstream committee. The Women's Officer in Region 2 acknowledged that there would be 'a fight on with some branches who will want to fight for the old structure, which although it sounds democratic, could be the cause of not being democratic'.

All self-organised groups submitted their constitutions for approval at the Regional Committee. Members of the Regional Committee in Region 2 challenged the proposals for the Women's Committee's structures on a number of points. As noted above, they objected to the absence of a motion-based forum. They also challenged the constitution of the Branch Equality Officers for Women, the Branch Women's Committee and the Regional Women's Committee. A senior woman activist explained why there had been such criticism of the constitutions:

> Because they got it wrong. They developed women's organisation and not self-organisation. The organisation is set up to control women lay members, rather than building up from principles of self-organisation. This constitution is seen as a watering down of self-organisation by paid officers to something more acceptable.

Two research findings seem to confirm this suspicion. First, the early meetings of the newly constituted Women's Committee had an orchestrated feel about them, with the Women's Officer playing a key role in proceedings (McBride, 1997). Secondly, the Chair of the Women's Committee noted in her interview that she suspected those 'who self-select for self-organisation as being there for the wrong reasons'. This is a surprising comment for a Chair of a Women's Committee to make and appears to confirm the senior activist's suspicions that self-organisation is being changed to something 'more acceptable'. However, interviews with a number of senior activists illustrated that these feelings were not too dissimilar from their own – despite their professed commitment to self-organisation.

The senior activist noted above believed that self-organisation was an important concept because 'it lets women meet in a less threatening environment'. However, she was also noted that self-organisation was open to abuse 'on grounds of accountability and take-over by factions because the oppressed are not open to challenge'. Another senior activist provided contradictory messages about self-organisation in her interview:

> Self-organisation is a channel for people to raise problems that specifically affect their group and a mechanism for getting people involved and confident ... I do worry that self-organisation encourages self-selection and is therefore not democratic ... Many members of self-organised groups do not put themselves forward for the same types of [mainstream] elections. Mainstream elections are open to everyone, not just those from a particular group. Self-organised groups are not part of the formal democratic mechanism of the union. If there are no women at a local level, where is the accountability of women to the branch?

Despite these misgivings, however, in the same interview, the activist noted that:

> Self-organisation should not be formalised too much. It enables people to participate who would not normally participate. I am in favour of it being informal and accepting what they say.

These interviews illustrate a paradox. On the one hand self-organisation is valued for being about freedom and self-expression, whilst on the other, it raises concerns (in the same people) about accountability. Briskin (1999) talks of an 'autonomy – integration' paradigm whereby self-organised groups are continually legitimising themselves through their autonomy from and integration into mainstream structures. This study of

UNISON confirms the universality of this balancing act. The targeting of all women in Region 1 provides autonomy but is likely to constrain integration at a later date. The targeting of women shop stewards in Region 2 seems to address these latent concerns about accountability but loses its legitimacy due to its perceived lack of autonomy. Briskin (1999) attributes this paradigm to the need for self-organised groups to organise within 'institutional realities'. At the time of this research, members and officers in Region 2 and elsewhere attributed this to self-organisation's lack of power. The preferred strategy of such groups and individuals was to enable women to access current power structures. This contrasted with the strategy of others, such as those in Region 1, who wished to generate new sources. The contrast in these strategies is seen most clearly in the debate about the activity and constituency of the National Women's Committee.

National Women's Conference

Encouraging activity at National Women's Conference

The interim Women's Committee in Region 2 submitted a motion to the 1995 National Women's Conference arguing for an alternative format for the Conference. The philosophy of developing women's skills through education and training programmes underpins the motion put forward by Region 2. The motion recognised the value of a motion-based forum for developing UNISON policy, but asked that the Conference recognise too, the 'valuable opportunity to enable women members to develop other forms of expertise and skill as well'. The motion finished:

> Conference therefore agrees that in future the National Women's Conference will be a combination of a motion based conference and activity based workshop in which workshops will be structured to: develop discussion on policy relating to the interests of women members; develop discussion on women members' needs within the organisation; build campaigning around issues relating to our women members' needs and facilitate skills training to meet needs identified by our women members.

As these extracts from different speakers illustrate, power was defined from two different perspectives. From one perspective, authority and influence derived from a motion-based conference:

> I'm not a child. I'm not here to be trailed from room to room. I don't want to be a sheep. I'm on a learning curve – not in a working group. We must learn to define our rights. We must learn to take our motions to the mainstream.

> The voice of women in UNISON is not heard in workshops – it's heard at women's conference.

> I want to gain experience on conference floor – conference skills are gained in conference.

> I'd rather be thrown into the lion's den at women's conference than at National Delegate Conference.

Where workshops were acknowledged as being valuable, it was argued that they were more appropriately conducted at branch, or regional level. Speakers who argued against this analysis noted that the National Women's Conference was just following the men's way of doing things, and that there was a need to break the mould, so that women could compete equally. Delegates were urged to think of those *not* at the Conference. Supporters argued that Conference was 'missing an ideal opportunity for education'. These extracts illustrate a different definition of power and questioned the nature of women's participation:

> I want to move away from old traditions. Shouldn't be putting women on the rostrum. Do we have to be so formal, bureaucratic? Policy can be formulated in workshops. More women can take part. It's difficult to give training at a motion-based conference.

> Totems – empowerment and enablement – if we are not about thinking of other women – then what are we about? I don't like the attitude 'if it's good enough for the boys, it's good enough for us' – well, I don't agree – I want something better. Some women are too busy jumping up and down to help others.

The motion to include activity-based workshops in the National Women's Conference was lost, and the decision was greeted with cheers. This response seemed to confirm everything the women had said about the motion-based conference being an inappropriate way of moving forward. Arguments had been put for and against the motion, but there had been no opportunity for discussion and finding a middle way.   The Women's Officer from Region 1 noted that:

> The Conference is not supportive to women. It is a very aggressive culture, ideology. Some women very familiar with constitution and battered [other] women into the ground ... Some regions are working on old NALGO organisation, they want the right to go to Conference irrespective of what that means ... The National Women's Conference would be bigger than the sovereign body ... But women feel that they are not important and this is because the debate has not been explained. They are wasting energy and time fighting for resources. They need to consider working objectives, long term strategy and making proportionality work and creating the means of enabling women to acquire the skills they need when they go into the real vipers nest.

Region 2, and their supporters, lost their argument for workshops at the National Women's Conference but their arguments against a larger National Women's Conference found support in the mainstream.

Determining the constituency of the National Women's Conference

In the opening address of the first National Women's Conference in 1994, the Conference was described as:

> A planning conference – an opportunity to develop proposals for permanent structures which could build on the best from the three partner unions and which would enable and encourage maximum participation by women in the union. (Address to Conference by Chair of National Women's Committee)

Each region was limited to sending 30 delegates to the 1994 National Women's Conference, making a total delegation of about 400.   A number of motions at the 1994 National Women's Conference condemned this limitation and it is understood that these debates took up a considerable amount of conference time.   The general feeling was that the Women's Conference should be branch based and that the opposition to this was raised in terms of cost considerations, and questions as to where the money was coming from to pay for a larger conference. One delegate attracted a great deal of support when she noted that the £1 million figure that had been mentioned as being 'too much', represented '£1 per women member'. After considerable debate, the 1994 National Women's Conference agreed that a future conference would be:

- branch delegated;
- branch representation to be at least 50 per cent of the branch's entitlement of delegates to Annual Conference; and at least one delegate per merged or unmerged branch;
- motion-based and a policy-making body.

Later in the year, the NEC advised the National Women's Committee that 'because of National Delegate Conference decisions on budgets and subscription rates, the size and funding for the conference would be restricted' (UNISON, 1994f, p. 6).

In response, the National Women's Committee asked the NEC to at least agree to a grouping of branches, in line with arrangements for National Delegate Conference (NDC). It was estimated that this would provide a delegation of approximately a thousand women members. This was rejected by the NEC who argued that the funding could not exceed the sum allocated for the 1994 Conference, and therefore limited the delegation to the 1995 National Women's Conferences to 500 women.

However, whilst some women argued that women's participation was being severely curtailed, others feared that separate organising was in danger of becoming an end in itself. A debate at the 1995 NDC provides an illustration of these different views. This is an extract of a motion that was passed at the 1995 National Women's Conference and submitted to the 1995 National Delegate Conference:

> This Conference is appalled over the low priority given to this Women's Conference by the NEC. Conference believes that future Women's Conferences should be representative of women throughout the union. Only direct branch representation can achieve this. Proportionality will not be achieved unless adequate resources are devoted to UNISON's women's organisation. This Conference therefore instructs the NWC to:

1) make strong representation on behalf of women members in UNISON, that decisions taken by democratic vote at Women's Conference are adhered to.

2) seek to ensure that National Women's Conference are, in future, both democratic and truly branch based.

Before discussing the Conference debate, it is worth considering several points in this motion. The motion notes that it is making a strong representation 'on behalf of women members' and makes the connection between women's organisation and proportionality. However, whilst the National Women's Conference can make decisions about its own policies, they were arguably naive in insisting that 'decisions taken by democratic vote at Women's Conference are adhered to' within the rest of the union, and this clause provided an immediate vehicle for rejecting the whole motion.

A speaker democratically elected from the National Women's Conference presented the motion to the National Delegate Conference. The first speaker in open debate spoke against the motion. She noted that exclusion happens at any conference and that self-organisation was not an end in itself. To applause she noted that, 'we won't need self-organisation at the end of the day because this conference will have the right number of women.'

The NEC opposed the motion. Opposition from the NEC was on two counts: sovereignty of the National Delegate Conference, and the role of the National Women's Conference. To begin with, the (female) NEC speaker reminded Conference that the NDC was the sovereign decision-making body and that the NEC was not able to give any such assurance that decisions made by the National Women's Conference would be adhered to. The NEC member then argued for the need for '2000 women at the National Delegate Conference, *not* at the Women's Conference. Women want *real* power. Vote for women, vote for real power in UNISON, vote against this motion.'

The speech by the NEC member was a very powerful one that was delivered with great confidence and conviction. This presentation made a strong contrast with the relative inexperience of the representative of the National Women's Conference who proposed the motion. Another woman active in women's self-organisation tried to clarify the position:

We are not asking for a conference as large as the National Delegate Conference but how can 500 women represent two-thirds of 1.3 million members? This is not democratically based. A promise was given to the National Women's Committee that a branch-based committee could be held, but then because of finance, they were told they could not. What message does this send out to women? I urge you to vote for this motion.

After a brief exchange of views the motion was put to the vote and the Conference voted against the motion, thus rejecting one of the motions that had been agreed at the National Women's Conference.

The debate about the National Women's Conference illustrates the different definitions of power within UNISON. It is interesting to note that a representative of the NEC should state that 'real power' is at the NDC. Can we assume therefore that self-organisation has no power within UNISON? Does this mean that the Women's Officer in Region 2 who believes that self-organisation has no power is right? Power is not mentioned in the rule book, but perhaps the indication of intent is shown in its provision that self-organised groups should 'work within the established policies, rules and constitutional provisions of the Union' (UNISON, 1993, p. 20). This debate has illustrated that the NDC is the supreme decision-making body of the union. It can give no guarantees that the decisions of the National Women's Conference will be adhered to. Indeed, the timing of the Conference meant that in two out of three years, no motions from the National Women's Conference were admissible to the Agenda. Of the two National Women's Conference motions submitted to the NDC one was rejected and one was accepted. All of this does seem to confirm that 'real power' is at the NDC. The consequence of this is that 'real power' can only be attained through one's activism at the branch level, since to attend the NDC, one needs to be elected from within one's branch.

Summary and discussion

Although constrained within rule-book responsibilities, the women's structures do have autonomy to develop their own roles, structures and constitutions. These case studies illustrate how this autonomy has led to very different interpretations, objectives and structures for women's organisation within two UNISON regions. The extent of this difference can be illustrated by the absence of 'self-organisation' in the constitution of Region 2. Whilst this might be an effect of developing a 'brownfield' organisation, it has a number of implications for the pursuance of women's interests within UNISON.

An important difference between the two regions relates to the access each provides for women members. The structures in Region 1 are specifically designed to include all women and do not prescribe women's activity within the union. In contrast, the structures in Region 2 are specifically designed around branch women shop stewards and mirror the representative structures within the mainstream union. In Region 2, separate organising is definitely structured as a means to an end. The ultimate aim of women-only structures in Region 2 is the long-term mobilisation of women into mainstream representative structures within the union. From this perspective, the two strategies for identifying women operate in a complementary manner in Region 2. However, whilst this philosophy provides a link between women's interests and women's concerns this is not how it is perceived by the mainstream Regional Committee. Underpinning their criticism were fears that the structure was excluding women members and facilitating officer control of the women's structures. However, whilst a study of the women's committee provides some justification for these fears, this arises through short-term relationships and is not derived from the structure itself. Indeed, given the need for greater participation at a local level (as illustrated in Chapter 6), focusing women's organisation around the branch is likely to lead to a much stronger women-led union.

Whilst the women's structures in Region 1 challenged the male model of trade unionism, at the time of my research, women's self-organisation was not challenging the status quo (or male power). Whilst the women's structures in Region 2 are an adaptation of the male standard, their development from a branch-representative base could ensure that they are less susceptible to criticism on the grounds of accountability and thus more likely to challenge the status quo within the union. Indeed training women to 'run the union' is the professed intention of the Women's Officer.

8 Making a Difference in Local Government?

The previous chapters have shown how the rule-book commitments to proportionality, fair representation and self-organisation have been implemented in practice. This chapter deals with the operation of proportionality, fair representation and self-organisation within the specific location of the Local Government Service Group (LGSG). Approximately 800,000 members of UNISON work in local government. One-third of these members are manual and craft workers, the remainder administrative, clerical or professional. Approximately 65 per cent of members in this service group are women. The experience of women in local government is often very different to that of men.

The following brief review of local government employment relates to the context of the research period 1993–1995. The Conservative Government made a two-pronged attack on local government during the 1980s and 1990s. Through increased centralisation, central Government forced local government to be a purchaser, rather than a provider of services. It also introduced Compulsory Competitive Tendering (CCT) for manual staffs, later extended to professional services. These two actions led to the fragmentation of employment units at a local level, providing potential for employers to break from national collective bargaining. As noted in Chapter 2, Fairbrother (1996) argues that local organisation and decision making has led to a renewal of workplace unionism based on forms of participatory democracy. However, in his review of union responses to the contracting-out of manual services, Colling (1995) argues against this analysis. He notes that CCT places too many demands on local activists who become increasingly caught up with the bureaucracy of the contracting process. In his argument, Colling (1995) refers to another restriction on workplace unionism: that of 'extremely uneven and gendered distribution of bargaining power' which led to women enduring the 'most disruption and the most severe cuts in terms and conditions'.

The detrimental impact of CCT on women is confirmed by the 1995 Equal Opportunities Commission (EOC) Report (Escott and Whitfield, 1995). This highlights the two-tier service evolving in local government, which divides permanent and casual staff, full-time and part-time staff, and men and women. The authors looked at four (manual) services subject to CCT in local authorities from September 1993 to March 1994. Escott and Whitfield noted the variation between the implementation of CCT in refuse collection (predominantly male workers), building cleaning and education catering (predominantly female workers). Building cleaning had been most affected by CCT and private contractors have won over half the contracts since 1989 (UNISON, 1995b). This sector saw a dramatic increase in the number of part-time and temporary staff, fewer overtime opportunities, increased productivity not being financially rewarded and drastic cuts in women's take-home pay. This was in contrast to refuse collection, which saw a smaller number of contracts go to private companies, authorities maintaining national rates and improving bonus schemes to take account of productivity and work intensification. There was no increase in part-time or temporary workers in refuse collection.

Across all four sectors, Escott and Whitfield (1995) reported that total female employment fell by 22 per cent and male employment by 12 per cent. In addition, research shows that female-dominated services accounted for over 90 per cent of the surpluses generated by in-house service organisations in the case-study authorities. This led Escott and Whitfield (p. 178) to argue that 'low paid women workers are effectively subsidising council expenditure and council taxpayers in general.' The extension of CCT to white collar services and the potential for women to lose out, once again, was noted by the EOC report. Escott and Whitfield estimated that approximately 100,000 women in white-collar jobs could be affected by CCT, 75 per cent who work full-time and 80 per cent of whom work in the lower grades. Given that men and women are segregated into jobs with differing rates of pay, the authors warned that women's rates could be reduced to match those in the private sector, whereas men's will remain the same, or increase to match those available in the private sector. (Although the election of a Labour Government in 1997 saw the replacement of Compulsory Competitive Tendering (CCT) with a performance management system known as 'Best Value' (IRS, 1998; Labour Research, 1999), CCT was a major concern during the research period.)

New sources of authority and influence have been generated for individual women on the Local Government Service Group Executive (LGSGE). Women took 73 per cent of the directly elected seats in the first election, although this male/female composition was slightly reduced (to 66 per cent women) when the indirectly elected seats were taken into account. As noted in Chapter 4, women contested and won a number of general seats and in three of the 13 regions, all three representatives were women. The proportion of women on the SGE represents a dramatic increase in the number of women representatives on the national executives of the former partner unions. This can be seen in the composition of the interim sector committees prior to the first SGE election. The Administrative, Professional, Technical and Clerical (APT&C) interim sector committee (primarily former NALGO members) consisted of 25 per cent women and the Manual & Craft (M&C) interim sector committee (primarily former NUPE members) consisted of 35 per cent women.

Past political processes that led to over-representation by men have been altered. However, representation is only part of the political process. It is necessary to know the extent to which changed political processes have lessened inequality (Bachrach and Baratz, 1970). Over a longer time period, it is important to look at the policy outcomes for men and women in Local Government. In the short term, I was looking at two main indicators of a lessening of inequality between men and women. The first indicator was the presence of women's voices on the committee. The second was the extent to which gender differences were made more visible and male norms were challenged (Briskin and McDermott, 1993b). Material was collected from attending five committee meetings of the national LGSGE, the national conference and regional LG committee meetings in Region 1. I interviewed activists and paid officers associated with each committee and analysed associated documentary evidence. In some sections of the chapter it has been useful to use names, but in each case this is not the person's real name.

The chapter presents a mixed picture of participation by individual women and the representation of women as a group. First, the chapter examines women's voices on the national SGE and notes how they are silenced. Second, the chapter provides illustrations of the gender-neutral nature of local government issues. Third, the chapter notes those situations in which women's voices were heard and a gendered analysis pursued. The chapter concludes that UNISON's strategy for gender democracy is too reliant on individual women and ignores the needs of women as an oppressed social group.

Women's voices

I made detailed notes at each of the five LGSGE meetings I attended and analysed 16 debates that resulted in formal proposals and decisions. Approximately 38 lay members were at each meeting, two-thirds of whom were women. Although women participated in all of these 16 debates, they only spoke an equal number of times, or more than men did, in six of these debates. I have attributed this to at least three causes.

Inequality of experience

There are 49 members of the Service Group Executive (SGE), which makes a very large committee meeting when everyone is present. Half of the members were completely new to local government meetings at national level. Of these 24 completely new members, 22 were women, the vast majority of whom had been elected to low-paid women's seats. This led to a disparity of previous experience amongst men and women. Only a third of the women on the new committee had had previous experience at a national level, compared with almost 90 per cent of the men. Thus, if it is easier for previously active members to know the issues, deal with the paperwork, and speak in ensuing debates, it could be argued there is an inherent bias against women speaking on the national SGE. In her discussion of the paradoxes of participation, Phillips (1991) talked of meetings being monopolised by those 'already favoured with wealth, education and power. After observing five SGE meetings, I would certainly add 'previous experience' to the list indicated by Phillips.

Only four of the newly active women were speaking at the meetings I attended, so it could be argued that women's previous experience has important implications for women's access to decision making. However, since M&C members make up at least half of the newly active women, it could have unfortunate implications for manual workers, and low-paid women too. Since male manual workers were not able to win any of the general seats on the SGE, their only form of representation on the 1995 Committee was through women occupying the low paid women's seats, one general seat, and two representatives from the M&C Sector

Committee. During my period of study, three of these 15 M&C members were contributing to debates of the national SGE. The SGE meetings I attended were the first meetings of the substantive committee and a considerable number of women on the committee had limited experience at this level of union structure. It could be that men and women's contributions will alter to reflect the growing experience of the women members. Certainly, the SGE were making efforts to facilitate members' full participation in the proceedings. The officers developed an induction programme, and introduced an informal mentoring system for new members. An interviewee went on one of the training courses and noted that it was 'very, very helpful'. With the exception of one man, all 20 participants were women. The interviewee noted that a number of women attending the course were in the same position as herself which was obviously of some comfort to her.

The service group is also structured to ensure that much smaller committees get involved in specific issues. Taking CCT as an example, it is possible to illustrate how these smaller committees work. CCT is the remit of the CCT/Privatisation Working Party that consists of six members. Informal processes have ensured that women occupy half the seats (two of whom are newly active), and the seats are split evenly between M&C and APT&C members. Membership is via the SGE or the main Sector Committees and a motion to include regional representatives was lost. Arguments for smaller groups relate to their efficiency, and their supportive nature. A senior activist noted:

> The mechanisms of work progression are different with the use of working parties which are smaller. More contribute, particularly women. Most business is generated by a small group of people, and the key negotiating body for single status is an example of 'good practice'. Everyone is at a similar level of information, discussions are behind closed doors (the best way of generating ideas is for individuals to talk freely), and it is possible to use 'away days'.

However, whilst it may just be a question of time before the newly active women start contributing in relation to their numbers, certain institutional practices might underpin the continued marginalisation of women – particularly those from the former NUPE. The first relates to inequalities of facilities between APT&C and manual members as described by three low-paid women members of the SGE.

Inequality of facilities

Sally is the branch secretary for 1700 members who work across a number of different sites. Sally is a part-time worker (20 hours per week), fully seconded on union duties. At the time of our interview she was working from home. Sally noted that working from home is hard work since everything must be done manually and without recourse to a secretary. The physical fragmentation of the members across the City, with few (if any) central workplaces, means that any consultation with the membership must be achieved through the post. She noted:

> The computer is still in the box; the photocopier is in the small bedroom; the typewriter remains in the box until I need it, and I am learning to type. I do the membership records manually – which is hard work. It is very time consuming. It is easier for me because I have the use of a car. My colleague [who covers half of the area] does not have a car and relies on public transport.

Some days Sally has meetings all day, sometimes she has meetings in the evenings from 6 to 10 pm. She noted that working at home is a trap, because there is no escape. She takes telephone calls all day, every day, and may well do about 60 hours a week (three times her part-time hours). She noted that sometimes her telephone bill could be up to ten pages long. She receives telephone calls on Saturdays, Sundays, Bank Holidays and at Christmas. These are all days on which some of her members may well be working and they justify their calls with 'I pay my subs every week, I should be able to get some action.'

These comments echoed those of two other low-paid women on the national SGE. Susan works in a school canteen and has few facilities. She feels that this puts her at a disadvantage in relation to her APT&C colleagues. Although she has access to a 'pay-as-you-go' school fax, this is not available when the office closes. She has access to a photocopier but this is seven miles away. Although she uses the facilities of another union at her workplace, her home telephone bill includes much UNISON work. She noted that it is easy to forget calls that have been made on union work, and consequently not claim for them. In addition, it is not convenient to make telephone calls at work, and no one can contact her if she is in a meeting. Her request for a mobile telephone has not been taken up. Susan travels a lot on union business, often at night-time, often cross-country, she feels that a mobile telephone would give her a sense of security should her car break down. Janet, another low-paid woman member on the SGE, also does her union work from home. Her branch office is five miles away, she travels there by public transport. Like Sally, Susan and Janet type their own work and need typing facilities. All three women noted that typing letters and photocopying documents are major parts of the job.

Both Susan and Janet contrasted their lack of facilities to the resources available in former NALGO offices. Like Sally, they find the circulation of material to members makes a lot of work for them. Even obtaining the postage is a problem. Although there are pre-paid envelopes available for some mail-outs, on most occasions they need to buy sheets of stamps at a time, which is quite expensive, and which they have to pay for initially. Another difference relates to time-off facilities for manual members. Susan works from 8 am to 1 pm, but because no one extra will be provided to cover any of her absences, or no extra time will be provided, the rest of her canteen will have to double-up to get the work done in the same time period: 'The member takes time off for a meeting, is not replaced, and then the same amount of work needs to shared by the smaller number of members who remain.'

A Local Government branch secretary in Region 1 confirmed this when she noted the implications of CCT for fair representation:

> Who is elected and who turns up is the key issue. This may be a problem of working commitments. If in a DSO, then absence will be letting down the team ... Even though there is time-off written into contract for union, you never know how contract will perform in practice. Every one of [branch] officers (except one) is in a DSO, and when one doesn't turn up for work, it creates problems.

Susan and Janet are both single parents and live on a very tight budget. They both felt that certain members and officers did not understand what low pay meant 'even when you say'. They believe that better-paid members and officers just 'don't understand how low paid we are'. Since neither Susan or Janet has a float, they must perform a delicate balancing act with their monies in order to fund their union activities. Although the money will be reimbursed eventually, it obviously gives them some difficulty, as they have to dip into their own funds that they are putting by for large expenses, such as holidays or bills, and then wait for UNISON to reimburse them.

Silencing of working-class voices

Despite good intentions, the use of smaller working groups has an unfortunate fall-out for the remainder of members on the SGE. The first is a perception that an 'inner cabal' operates the national group. The second is that since much work is undertaken in smaller working groups, the SGE revolves around officers' papers and formal discussions, with a huge agenda generalising across the whole of union business. The word 'huge' to describe the agenda is not an understatement. Very often in the meetings the documentation was at least 1 cm thick, requiring several hours of non-stop reading. One new member noted that 'The paperwork is difficult to understand, and if I had known what was involved, I would never have volunteered. I am learning too many things in a short time.'

An interview with Sally gave me an insight into what it is like for a low-paid woman who had never stood for a national seat before. Extracts from a semi-structured interview with her graphically illustrate the 'newness' of the role she has undertaken and the manner in which she feels excluded and intimidated. Two issues were of particular concern to her. The first related to perceptions of her colleagues as former NALGO members. The second related to the accepted practice (amongst her former NALGO colleagues) of writing a feedback report for the regional committee:

> I felt very isolated at the first weekend of the SGE at Chester. I felt – and still do – that people are not friendly and that they are people who have been on committees for a long time. I only really gelled with one person. Elaine [one of the regional representatives] was not there and David [the other regional representative] provided no support. He asked 'will I write the report?' I did not know we had to do a report, so I just replied 'yes, go ahead.' I was not given a look at the report until it came up at the regional meeting.

Sally noted that she did not travel in her former partner union (NUPE), and found her first trip to London rather daunting. At the time of our interview, it seemed that she still did not enjoy the journey to London. Since the other regional representatives travel down the previous day, she travels on her own. At the first meeting of the SGE, Elaine met her at the station but has not repeated this. Sally said 'She must think I know my way now.' Sally described her experience of the national SGE meetings:

> Elaine and David converse all the time and I feel left out. Elaine told me she would write the report, and that I could do it next time, but I told her 'no I won't', because I did not feel that I would know how to ... Elaine and David have given me no support at all. It's because they are ex-NALGO members. I think this makes a difference. I don't see the reports [of the SGE meeting] before they go before the regional committee' ... David and I talk but I still feel that he is above me.

A senior activist talked about the problems created by low-paid women's seats, noting that NUPE women activists tended to be only active at branch level, and might just be a steward at that level. She noted that the unskilled women had less confidence and feels that that aspect of the structure does not work:

> [The reservation of low-paid seats] sends out the message that UNISON wants low-paid women involved but I do not believe they are yet ready. Training and support mechanisms have been provided for low-paid women on the committee and I hope the women will stand again and become active at that level.

Sally did stand again for the low-paid women's seat. However, whilst the Chair was concerned that the women were only active at branch level, interviews with two low-paid women on the SGE illustrated a different viewpoint:

> In many ways APT&C don't have a clue about what is going on job wise. But they don't think manuals have any 'nous' and always underestimate you. They can be very patronising at all levels: regional, national, local. They treat us as if we have not been in a union before, never sat on regional or local committees.

Such patronisation is articulated in the words of a key activist who noted that:

> The SGE is only able to go at the speed of the slowest. The reservation of low-paid women's seats is not helping the bodies they are on. Finding ways of making them comfortable – whilst I accept it is a job that you have to do

– still means that it is preventing getting on with other things. If you are going to be active at the top, you need to be experienced.

Whilst some of the low-paid women would disagree with this assessment, it could be justified by Sally's experience: 'Voting is sometimes a problem when I don't know what they are talking about. I don't understand everything, but know that it is exactly the same for some other women.'

The observation that the SGE can only go 'at the speed of the slowest' conflicts with observations of low-paid members. From interviews, it would appear that 'self-censorship' is one reason for women's lack of voice. Despite the Chair's endeavours to be facilitating and in the words of one interviewee 'waiting for someone to speak from the manual side', one low-paid woman noted:

> The APT&C members speak again, and again, and again – going round and round in circles. Manuals won't speak for the sake of it, or repeat something already said, they do not speak because there is nothing left to say. We've all learnt to keep matters short, since members always have to get back to work. If you speak to manuals for ten minutes, then those members will have to work ten minutes over.

Indeed, whilst a workshop discussion at an SGE Policy Seminar noted the different levels of involvement by some members, it also noted:

> There was also a view that the higher level of involvement by some other members was equally a problem, as it was this that caused the problem of some Service Group Executive members being unwilling or unable to contribute fully.

The structure of the service group at national level means that women directly elected to the SGE are involved in broader strategic issues, hearing report back and discussing constitutional matters. There are few opportunities to discuss occupation-specific matters and only a limited number are involved in the working parties on CCT and single-status. Added to the capacity of some members to speak 'for the sake of it', several low-paid members noted that they were often 'dead bored' with issues at the SGE meetings. In addition, by being concerned that low-paid women were only active at branch level, key activists were in danger of devaluing branch-based experiences and ignoring the very different experiences that low-paid manual workers have.

The definition of norms

The second indicator of change within UNISON was the extent to which differences of gender were made more visible and male norms were challenged (Briskin and McDermott, 1993b). A national paid officer indicated the scale of change required in the bargaining agenda

> The bargaining agenda is male dominated, numerically and culturally. Pay is seen as the issue – but there are other issues equally important – for example, number of hours that some members want to come to top of table. Concentrating on pay for part-time workers is sometimes inappropriate because more money triggers a benefit trap. But this is difficult for national negotiators because they are not there to only support those in the poverty trap.

A UNISON membership survey of part-time workers in cleaning and catering services (in Newcastle) indicated three clear priority areas: health and safety, pay, and working conditions. The survey also highlighted the extent to which part-time workers were the holders of multiple jobs, and therefore working far longer hours than 'part-time' might suggest. Multiple-job holding had a number of implications for the women, and UNISON. The survey revealed that for many women, their UNISON job contributed only part of their income, and therefore UNISON could only marginally affect their working and economic lives. The survey also showed that the cost of travelling was a disproportionate drain on women's financial resources. For example, for those with two jobs in cleaning, travelling could cost up to £8.86 per week, which represented 9 per cent of the average weekly income. Travelling was also costly in terms of time, and the average time spent travelling by cleaning staff was 3 hours, 9 minutes per week. I asked a paid officer whether these results were likely to be generalisable across the UK:

> It might be due to high male unemployment, but nonetheless it is an equality issue. Part-timers possibly prefer buying back hours - would prefer less hours than more money in their purse ... There is also an interest in

developing people in jobs ... Facilities for elder care are the biggest issue –
more than childcare.

Material to help activists cope with Compulsory Competitive Tendering
emphasised the tendency for the male experience to be taken as 'the
norm'. The main emphasis has been the provision of information to
branches (see UNISON, 1994d and 1995b) and campaigning against CCT
at a national level. Whilst negotiations and statutory remedies have
brought a number of rewards, it could be construed as 'closing the stable
door after the horse has bolted'. Although the national guide to
retendering in manual CCT (UNISON, 1995b) admitted that women
suffered disproportionately from the first round of tendering, it offered
little practical advice to reduce this the next time round. It noted that
'pre-tender cuts to wages and conditions should not be accepted', but
gave no indication in the in-house bid preparation as to what should be
done. It did not spell out, for example, the analysis of one key activist
that female members in cleaning and catering suffered more because they
are 'not traditionally militant, they work part-time, and they are difficult
to organise'. Nor did it note that dustbin workers can 'get what they want
because they have more opportunity to withdraw labour'. Nor did it
indicate in 'Lessons learnt in the first round of tendering' what this
interviewee said about choices being made in the first round that were
detrimental to women:

> When DSO [Direct Services Organisation] managers were looking at
> competition, they would inevitably cut those wages which the labour market
> would accept. The private employer does not have to pay the retainer for
> the school holiday, so the DSO will try and recoup the cost of providing it
> through cutting the number of hours worked. In the event, the local
> authorities were cutting more than they needed to, the competition was not
> that fierce, or sometimes there was no competition. Local branches were
> frightened into accepting worse deals. There was bad advice within the
> union and a number of 'dreadful deals' where too much was sold.

Two women noted the union's emphasis on restraining cuts. One paid
officer noted: 'Decisions have been taken on the false premise that men's
jobs should be protected. Deals are done for the protection of the greater
number of jobs – not out of malice, but false assumptions of value of
work.'

However, the paid officer also confirmed that men's conditions had worsened too, but in a different way. The officer noted that although the hours of ground maintenance staff and refuse collectors had been increased, they had been given annualised hours contracts, which had resulted in a net loss of terms and conditions.

The UNISON guide to white-collar CCT (UNISON, 1994d) discussed union organisation in some detail and noted that 'areas of the workforce that have no steward or have weak organisation are more at risk than well organised groups.' However, the distinction was not made between the experience of male and female members. As noted above, Escott and Whitfield (1995) reported their fears that women stood to lose more from contracting than men since comparisons with private rates of pay meant savings were possible in their jobs. Although the UNISON guide came out before the EOC report, it is unlikely that this possibility had not been noticed within the union beforehand. A lay activist noted that authorities could package services for white-collar CCT on a gendered basis. She also noted that no advice had been issued on this matter and nothing was being said explicitly about protecting women. Another woman noted:

> No one has followed through what is happening to women employees. Emphasis has been on professional jobs, whereas the women do many of the support jobs. There is no information on what has happened to women. Traditionally, the public sector has been a good employer to women, and these conditions may not be available in the private sector.

An officer noting that the union did not do enough to raise women's awareness, reflected that 'there is a difficult balance to strike because the question might be asked, why be in the union?' Without a gendered analysis and appropriate action at a local level, the danger is that history will repeat itself and the EOC will reporting on the gender impact of white-collar CCT in local government in two years time. Since the national service group had been established for less than a year, and the EOC report was published half-way through the research, it would be too early to pronounce that proportionality, fair representation and self-organisation had failed to put women's concerns at the forefront of the agenda. However, observations made during the research period suggest that it will be difficult to change in the immediate future. The first relates to responses to the EOC report.   The second relates to debates about single status.

Action against Compulsory Competitive Tendering

The EOC report (Escott and Whitefield, 1995) was the subject of much consideration within the service group.   The LGSGE organised a fringe meeting at their national Conference to discuss the report at which the authors would be present.   Few members attended the meeting.   This was in contrast to the number of members debating CCT in the hall immediately prior to the fringe meeting.   At a national level, debates concerning CCT appeared polarised around whether to take national strike action against employers' use of CCT.   The conference debate was gendered insofar as the EOC report was invoked in calls for a national strike ballot against CCT.   However, examples given of effective strike action were often those of refuse collectors which were taken as the norm with no acknowledgement that other jobs – particularly those performed by women – often precluded effective action against employers.   This is not to say that women did not take part in industrial action.

Women had taken action against CCT at a local level.   A branch secretary in Region 1 told me how 40 part-time women workers had lobbied a Council to ensure that there was no change in enhancement schemes for care assistants.   Likewise, women in Sheffield Libraries had successfully fought against the removal of national terms and conditions. The key difference was that calls for national days of action ignored the reality that many women did not work five days a week or indeed were not UNISON members for twelve months of the year.   A branch secretary of a Local Government manual branch in Region 1 noted:

> School meals and cleaning have term-time contracts only, so that each term workers leave, and then we have to pick them up again [when they return to work] ... We have tried to ensure proper protection for term-time workers but only when they become employees again, can they become trade union members.

Single status

In the words of a UNISON leaflet, 'single status is about ending the artificial split between 'white collar' (APT&C), 'blue collar' (manual) and craft workers' terms and conditions'. A review of the equal opportunities aspects of Single Status by Hastings (1995) notes that 'It is recognized by both Sides that the current structures are open to challenge on "equal pay for work of equal value" grounds, and almost certainly on straightforward discrimination grounds also.'

After noting a number of different sources of unequal pay within the Local Government sector, Hastings notes that 'it is surprising perhaps, that there have not been many more discrimination and equal pay claims in the sector.' A briefing document circulated at a LGSGE meeting noted that 'equal opportunities will be at the heart of single status' and 'single status is being built on the principle of equal treatment for women, part-time workers, temporary workers, black workers, disabled workers and lesbians and gay men.' However, despite these prescriptions, there was no debate in SGE meetings of the implications of Single Status for women. The closest SGE discussions got to such issues was the tabling of a 6-page document that indicated UNISON's possible negotiating position. It included reference to job evaluation.

The paid officer introducing the document noted that UNISON had engaged an academic to provide advice on a new job evaluation scheme that would take account of equal pay and low pay. The officer indicated that job evaluation would be fundamental to the agreement, but that it would not be prescriptive. Of five options for job evaluation, the Single Status Working Group recommended that there should be a new agreed national job evaluation scheme, based on principles of equality, which should be available to both sides locally. There was little discussion of any of the contents of this document and certainly no discussion about the preferred job evaluation scheme option. Instead, the discussion related to the adverse effect of job evaluations on those most likely to lose out in a re-evaluation of jobs.

At no point during the period of my research was the issue of job evaluation discussed again. The implications of Single Status for women were not discussed in the women's structures and nor were they raised as a specific issue of concern by any of the LG women members I interviewed. Reference has already been made to the need to eradicate union complicity in the gendered segmentation of the labour market (Briskin and McDermott, 1993b), before unions go beyond 'letting women in'. On the face of it, this silence over an important issue for women could be seen as confirmation that the presence of more women on committees does not necessarily equate with more discussion of women's issues, and that structures and practices still exist which marginalise women. Some of this silence could be explained by the structure of the SGE that ensured that specific issues, such as Single Status, were the remit of specific working groups. However, this is only a partial explanation because the SGE did discuss some aspects of Single Status in considerable detail.

The brief discussion about job evaluation can be contrasted with the lengthy discussion of the consultation procedures for Single Status. The member starting the debate noted that 'The future of the union rests on getting this right. Its importance is secondary only to the development of UNISON.'

The consultation procedures were contained on one side of A4 paper. Three amendments were proposed to this paper and the committee took one hour to discuss them fully. This discussion illustrated the priority given to certain aspects of Single Status. It also illustrated the gender-neutral nature of some of the democracy debates within UNISON. One of the male members proposed that members should be consulted at branch level through a branch-based ballot. He argued that this was 'more reliable', and 'more democratic' since there was a lower return for postal ballots. Eight members opposed this, five were women, and three were manual and craft members. One of the manual and craft (male) members noted that 'not everyone has facilities to branch ballot'. Another manual and craft (female) member noted how impractical it was, given that some branches have up to a hundred workplaces, and many members do not work at the same time. One woman noted that her membership was spread over 60 miles, and another woman noted that some members have no workplace. However, despite these interventions by a number of women, it is interesting that the democratic process was discussed in terms of numbers, and not gender. At no point, did anyone discuss the fact that if the members most likely to be in fragmented workplaces were women, this would mean that women would be those most likely not to be included in the 'democratic process'.

Women and a gendered analysis

In the main, when they spoke on the SGE, women confirmed Cockburn's (1996) argument that women elected from a mixed constituency do not speak only for women. Regional mandates were quite strictly adhered to in some regions, so when women spoke, they were often representing the views of their region, or the sector group. Whilst this indicates the importance of identity groups having representation on the SGE, it should be noted that women also spoke about issues which were of particular concern to them as workers in education, school meals, or as organisers of members in fragmented workplaces. That is, although the groups of workers they spoke of were not specifically identified as women, it was usually the experiences of women to which they were referring. Notwithstanding the need to adhere to regional mandates, it would appear that identifying women as a sex category can lead to the discussion of women's concerns – where they are defined by occupation, rather than by gender. Unfortunately, there is a mobilisation of bias against these opportunities arising on a frequent basis. The limited discussion of women's concerns did not, however, mean that inequalities were not addressed within the service group.

UNISON's approach to CCT had been supplemented by recourse to remedies through statutory, or negotiating bodies, which have reaped a number of rewards. Examples include the negotiation of enhanced rates of pay for part-timers for weekend working (equal to full-timers), and persuading the government to change the regulations on Family Credit so that the hours of part-timers would not be averaged out over a year. A briefing document circulated to branches and regions after my research contained considerable discussion of equality issues. This provided a contrast with the silence I had noted concerning women and Single Status. The document notes that 'joint advice on equalities was the first part of the national agreement to be negotiated' (UNISON, 1996b, p. 3). A whole page (p. 5) is devoted to 'Equal Value'. The document notes that 'A key issue will be whether the agreed job evaluation scheme should be mandatory, i.e. applied in all authorities or whether it should be available for use locally.'

The document also notes that national employers want authorities to be free to choose whether to apply any scheme, giving them 'maximum flexibility over how posts are graded'. The next paragraph is particularly interesting, given that it seems to illustrate a move away from the previous recommendations on the job evaluation scheme:

> Views are mixed in UNISON, however the national negotiators are concerned that if applying the job evaluation scheme is optional, it will be

> very difficult to have a pay structure and to deliver consistency and equal value in grading within and across authorities. (p. 5)

Also printed on the page were four 'key questions' for members to discuss concerning the operation of a job evaluation scheme. The document also raised other issues that addressed the work of women. The document indicated the union's commitment to negotiating a new minimum wage rate (stated as £4.26 per hour). With regard to 'Working Time, Leave and Premium Pay' (p. 8), it noted the launch of UNISON's 'Equal Hours – Equal Pay' campaign and the encouragement of members to take equal pay tribunal cases. It noted its intention to use 'existing legal judgements to ensure equality of treatment for part-time workers in any single status agreement', and to negotiate 'improved career and training opportunities, with pay for all hours spent on courses'. It also noted that whilst current bonus earners 'must be protected':

> The manual agreement's code of guiding principles on bonus schemes is outdated and must not be imported into the new agreement ... The unions are seeking expert advice on the equal value questions and practical implications for direct service organisations. (p. 11)

Since this document was published after the end of my research I have not determined the source of this gendered analysis in the document. It is difficult to reconcile this level of attention with the absence of such gendered analysis in the SGE meetings. However, some sources are more likely than others to have determined this outcome. An obvious source of pressure would be the women on the SGE, but given the types of discussion, and levels of women's participation during the previous twelve months, this is not a likely source in such a short time period. Given that women's self-organisation does not have direct representation on the SGE and do not appear to have discussed this issue at a national level, the pressure from women's structures can be discounted. The pressure could have emanated from members of the Single Status and Pay Steering Group, or the Equalities Project Group of the SGE. The work programme of the latter group included the consideration of 'progress on single status at all stages and advice on the equalities dimension'. Again, however, this group had been established for a relatively short period of time.

The more likely source of a gendered analysis of Single Status is a female officer in the Local Government Service Group. Heery and Kelly (1988a and b) note that women paid officers were more likely to raise issues of concern to women. Whilst paid officers have not been the focus of this study, a number of women have referred to women officers (as opposed to Women's Officers) who have taken a key role in raising women's concerns. I discussed the raising of women's awareness in UNISON with a paid officer at national level. At the time of my research she believed that there was too much reliance on individual (female) officers in specific service groups raising, and addressing, women's concerns, citing the female officer in Local Government as an example. Given the less than proportionate nature of female employment in UNISON, this leaves a considerable gap for issues to be raised by members through mainstream committees, or women's structures. It also indicates the importance of building relationships between women paid officers and members in women's structures – an element not necessarily appreciated by both parties.

Interviews with two key women involved in the Local Government SGE illustrated their disappointment with initial liaison meetings with representatives from self-organised groups, and a scepticism about the value of women's self-organisation. A (female) paid officer noted her personal belief that self-organisation, as it was structured, was not appropriate for women in UNISON. This woman had gained the impression that the National Women's Committee was more interested in structural issues, and that they had no interest in bargaining issues. Indeed she felt that the women's structures did not relate to the needs of the ordinary member, which she found disappointing. However, she did note that perhaps it was too early to judge and that maybe discussions around structure would evolve to policy and national bargaining issues.

A key female activist on the SGE noted that 'there is a lot that could be done, but it is not being done.' The activist noted that the way round this was to involve representatives from self-organised groups in negotiations, but that it needed 'a radical challenge to get different people involved'. Another female paid officer noted the need for partnership between lay members in women's structures and paid officers. She said that 'when they work against each other it is disastrous and makes it very difficult to move forward on workplace issues.' She felt that there was an 'anti-officer feeling from certain people' on the National Women's Committee.

Summary and discussion

Chapters 4, 5 and 6 have shown how the concepts of proportionality and fair representation have encouraged representation by individual women as members of an oppressed social group. This chapter has addressed its impact on women as a group. Proportionality, fair representation and self-organisation should be part of the processes that ensure that CCT is not disproportionately detrimental to women and that Single Status improves women's position in the workplace. Through formal processes of proportionality, women are getting directly elected to the national SGE in numbers which were not attained before. However, this study has shown that access to decision-making bodies is not necessarily leading to a gendered agenda. There are a number of factors that underpin this contingent relationship.

The first point to note relates to women's access through proportionality. Women are directly elected to the SGE from a mixed constituency and, as noted by Cockburn (1996), women elected from a mixed constituency are not required to speak, or vote, specifically for women. The legitimacy of this strategy is underpinned by the fact that many SGE members appear to have a regional mandate, and indeed sit and vote in regional groups. Thus, on the SGE, women usually talk from a regional perspective or, when appropriate, a sector or occupational perspective. In this way, 'basic justice' is attained in terms of women's physical access to decision making. Women on the Local Government SGE did not participate in proportion to their numbers. Indeed, at the time of my research, men who occupied one-third of the seats were often dominating decision-making debates. Thus, physical presence is only one part of women's access to decision making. This study indicates, again, that women's full access to decision making is facilitated by previous experience. Phillips (1991) talks of the characteristics associated with a person's monopolisation of meetings. This study adds 'expertise' to that list.

Whilst it may well only be a question of time before newly active women fully participate in all debates, interviews and observations of the SGE members indicate that a number of predominant values and beliefs continue to marginalise them. One relates to what members talk about. When newly active women speak, they tend to speak about workplace issues, whereas when previously experienced women speak, they tend to speak about wider, policy-based issues. This could be a very useful combination. However, interviews and observations indicate that workplace-based discussions are not seen as a 'good thing' on national committees. Expertise is defined by wide knowledge of general issues. It is defined by writing reports, and reading and digesting pages of text. It is not defined in terms of the ability to self-censor the spoken word and make short concise contributions, nor is it defined in terms of knowledge of low pay and workplace issues. That it is not defined in terms of workplace issues supports the limited gendered analysis of issues. It is only when workplace issues are raised by *women* that women's experiences are fully articulated and distinguished from the experience of 'gender-neutral' members. On the whole, the wider, policy-based issues were not discussed from a gendered perspective. This was particularly noticeable in relation to discussions about trade union democracy, work organisation, and issues such as CCT and Single Status.

Earlier chapters have illustrated the extent to which democracy is defined in terms of the lay and paid-officer relationship and these findings were reiterated on the LGSGE. Pateman (1983) talked about democracy being discussed 'in abstraction from the private sphere of domestic life' and this can certainly be used to describe the manner in which many members of the SGE discussed democracy. No consideration was given to the extent to which women's ability to participate in union consultation exercises might be constrained by their domestic responsibilities. Moreover, democracy was perceived in abstraction from the experiences of manual, often women, members. These were experiences such as limited facilities time, limited administrative services and limited funds. In addition, these gender-neutral discussions of democracy often took up a considerable amount of time, creating another mobilisation of bias against the fuller discussion of women's concerns on the SGE.

These findings have a number of implications for women's future organisation within UNISON. The contrast between newly active and previous experienced women illustrates the importance of all women getting together and discussing issues of concern, so that newly active women can gain expertise, and previously active women can be reminded of the implications of women's work. This chapter also illustrates that the strategy which 'identifies women as an oppressed social group' is not, as yet, producing a gendered analysis of union issues. By their very nature, self-organised groups are supposed to define their own priorities, and in the first two years of UNISON, self-organised groups at national and regional level have been preoccupied with defining a role and obtaining resources for themselves. This has meant that not enough bridges have been built between individual women elected to mainstream committees and women operating within self-organisation. Where the women's group has acted as a pressure group, it has been in obtaining more resources for itself, rather than changing the nature of negotiations. This chapter also indicates that bridges need to be built between members of women's structures and women paid officers.

9 Making a Difference at Regional Level?

The previous chapter provides a mixed picture of the impact of proportionality and fair representation on political processes. On the one hand it showed how women's voices were silenced and male norms dominated discussions. On the other hand, it noted instances when male norms were challenged and women's voices were heard. The chapter concluded that a strategy which relied on the election of individual women was limited in its ability to radically change the political processes. It argued that the displacement of male norms and the din of other issues required representation of women as an oppressed social group. These themes are pursued in this study of regional structures in Region 2.

The function of the region is to operate in an intermediary role between branches and national levels of the union, and between different service groups. It also plays a co-ordinating role in relation to campaign strategies, and education and publicity activities. The region is divided into Regional Council and Regional Committee. All branches in the region are entitled to send delegate(s), and motions, to the Regional Council, which 'shall have power to make policy at Regional level and to do such other things as may be reasonably necessary to carry out its functions'. The Regional Committee is essentially the management committee of the Council and exercises the functions of the Regional Council between its meetings. It is at the regional level where the union pursues work and community interests that affect members and their families across all services.

New sources of authority and influence have been generated for both individual women and women as a group at regional level. Women took 80 per cent of the regional representative seats in the first Regional Committee election. In addition, a representative of the Women's Committee has a seat on the Committee. In common with observations of the Local Government structures, I looked at two main indicators of a lessening of inequality between men and women – the presence of women's voices and the visibility of gender differences. Material was collected from attending four Regional Committee meetings and four Regional Council meetings. I interviewed activists and paid officers operating in the region and analysed associated documentary evidence. This material was complemented with the material collected from the women's structures in Region 2.

The observation of this committee presents a useful comparison to that of the national service group committee. First, it illustrates how women's presence is directly translated into women's voices. Women are not silenced on this committee. Secondly, it indicates that gender differences are made visible on this committee. However, this again is a mixed picture. The visibility of some gender differences contrasts with the limited crossover of discussion between issues raised within the women's structure and those raised in the mainstream committees. The chapter indicates that this is a result of two processes. The first relates to the ineffectiveness of the institutional mechanisms for group representation. The second relates to the din of other issues.

Women's access to decision making at Regional Council

The study of the Regional Council indicated four elements in women's access to the decision-making arena: physically being there, being vocal, the quoracy of the meeting and knowing the 'rules of the game'. Delegations to the Council in Region 2 are required to represent proportionality in the branch. Forty per cent of attendees at the first AGM were women – more women will need to be sent from branches before proportionality is achieved at the Regional Council. Another aspect of women's access to decision making is women's participation in the proceedings and this was observed at four Council meetings. The meetings were held in a very large hall, were highly politically charged and felt quite different to the Council meetings attended in Region 1. On the whole, I felt these meetings would have dissuaded any but the most confident and experienced from taking part. This was despite the efforts of the (female) Regional Convenor to curtail calling out, interruption from the floor, and circular discussions. Despite this somewhat daunting debating environment, women contributed to all debates. My observations were similar to those identified by the monitoring of the first AGM by the Recruitment and Organisation sub-committee (McBride, 1997). Although the figures referred to each contribution and took no account that several speakers probably spoke more than once during the day, they illustrated the extent to which women participated in the Council. In particular, they indicated that ex-NALGO women and ex-NUPE women spoke proportionately more than their male colleagues in relation to the numbers of men/ women present. Thus, women's proportional access to the Regional Council was prescribed within the constitution, and although absolute proportionality had not yet been reached, women attending the Council were gaining access to all debates.

Women's access to decision making at Regional Committee

Women comprised 80 per cent of regional representative seats on the 1994/95 Committee and 70 per cent on the 1995/96 committee. In 1995, the Regional Convenor and Deputy Convenor were both women. In terms of women's active participation in the committee, women made up between 60 and 70 per cent of the four meetings attended by myself. On all occasions women contributed at least in proportion to their numbers. On one occasion women made 80 per cent of contributions, whilst comprising 60 per cent of the committee attendees. Reflecting on the Committee, the Chair of the Women's Committee noted that 'the Regional Committee is quite fair', and that women were 'not being held back at the Committee'. Another member noted that

> The level of participation in the Committee is quite good. I feel that most people speak, and that it is a comfortable committee ... The Regional Committee has moved on and matured politically. (Interview with 1995 committee member)

Asked whether an increase in the number of women at regional level had made any difference, a senior lay activist noted that

> Some women have had to come to terms with the fact that they are no longer 'special', and have had to roll up their sleeves and get on with things. This is a healthy situation. The Regional Committee is quite friendly, but this is due to the mixture of different [union] cultures, not because there are more women on the committee.

However, a breakdown of the contributions by women at Regional Committee revealed that not all women participated. On three occasions, approximately 60 to 70 per cent of women present spoke, which rose to 80 per cent at the last meeting attended by the author. One woman made up to one-fifth of all (male and female) contributions at the three meetings she attended. Perhaps more than anything, this illustrates the difference between newly active women, and women who are very experienced at participating within the union. Those women not participating were usually women new to the Regional Committee and women elected to low-paid women's seats (who were sometimes synonymous). The Regional Convenor noted:

> A number of local women are continuing to make contributions, but not all women contribute. I would like to see all debates shift – more of other debates – though this is not just true of women ... We should ask ourselves what do we mean by participation – do we mean that they have to speak? We should find out why [women] are not speaking – how else would you know?

However, a key (female) activist did not expect that the presence of more women would bring significant changes to the discussion of women's concerns. She noted:

> Women are breaking former alliances now. They are now freer to make alliances with other women of their own political persuasion, rather than forming alliances with other women, just because they are women. I do not feel the same compulsion to raise 'women's needs', as there are plenty of other women who will raise the issues.

This confirms Cockburn's (1996) argument that women from a mixed constituency are not obliged to speak on behalf of women. The one woman who is obliged to speak on behalf of women occupies the seat reserved for a representative of the Regional Women's Committee. During 1994/95 and 1995/96, the Chair of the Women's Committee took this seat. Interview material indicates that she is very clear about her obligation to speak on behalf of women:

> ...to progress wherever possible women's point of view. I feel that the committee's response is sympathetic and supportive – although one or two make me feel intimidated. I believe there is a unity developing amongst women on pensions, part-time low-paid workers, and meeting times. I spoke for women at the Regional Committee when I noted the undesirability

of evening meetings for women. Men not having been in that position never had to think about it, but once it was put to them, they related it to their partners ... My role is 'the voice' of the women of the region.

The constitution of the Women's Committee specifically mentions its role in the 'organisation, participation and representation of women members'. Whilst participants in both structures expect to 'make a difference', it is only the women's structure that is specifically constituted to make a difference for women. The importance of this brief can be illustrated by an analysis of the election addresses of 15 nominees to the mainstream Regional Committee. Each nominee talked about the need to organise members and fight job cuts but only two nominees distinguished women as a specific category of members hit by the cuts.

The observation of structures in Region 2 would indicate that proportionality, fair representation and self-organisation have altered political processes between men and women. A considerable number of individual women gained access to all debates in proportion to their membership of the union. In addition, women as a group are represented on this committee. The next section addresses the extent to which gender differences were made visible and the concerns of women as a group are heard in UNISON.

The visibility of gender differences

Briskin and McDermott (1993b) argue that unions' complicity in the gendered segmentation of the labour market, and union support for traditionalist ideologies about women's work, need to be addressed before unions are transformed beyond the simple concept of 'letting women in'. As noted in the previous chapter, many of the debates of the Local Government Service Group Executive (LGSGE) were gender neutral and assumed that the experience of male members was the norm. Gender differences were more visible in the regional committee and council debates. Women were often identified as being the subject of different experiences. Examples include the regional debate on the National Minimum Wage (discussed later in this chapter), the gender of paid officers in UNISON taking the severance package, and pension rights. A recurring topic related to regional responses to women's job cuts.

Although only two of 15 nominees identified women as specific victims of job cuts, women were often distinguished from men when discussing proposed activity against job cuts in the region. One such dispute concerned the sacking of a hundred low-paid women cleaners, who had been dismissed after the privatisation of a contract by an employer in the Higher Education sector. Representatives of the Higher Education service group spoke at the Regional Committee and called for UNISON to boycott the hiring of venues within the region as a way of pressurising the employers into taking remedial action. Members calling for this action noted the tension between encouraging the participation of low-paid women through reserved seats and not supporting their cause. The vote to continue the boycott was carried by the Regional Committee and it continued until the ending of the dispute.

A low-paid female member who had spoken at the Regional Committee on this issue felt that this had been one of the few things she had been able to pursue from the workplace to Regional Committee and see things happen as a consequence of her input. So, for her, she did indeed feel that she 'made a difference'. She had intervened at these meetings and talked on behalf of members who, like herself, were low-paid cleaners.

However, although gender was more visible on this committee, this did not necessarily mean that the concerns of the women's group were discussed. First, the same issues were sometimes analysed from different perspectives. Second, the concerns articulated by women in the women's structures did not make their way onto the Regional Committee.

Different perspectives

Several issues were discussed in the mainstream Regional Committee and the Women's Committee and provided useful insights into the different perspectives of women in UNISON. One issue was the dispute (mentioned above) concerning large numbers of women cleaners. This was discussed to a much greater extent on the mainstream Regional Committee than within the Women's Committee. Indeed, it was only the implications of the boycott for the hiring of rooms for future meetings that was discussed, not the plight of the women themselves. Reference was made above to the low-paid women member who had campaigned for a continuation of the boycott. Although she was a member of the

Regional Women's Committee, she did not receive any encouragement from this forum for her stand. Indeed, she told me that she had been criticised by the Women's Officer because she had spoken out against the Regional Secretary in relation to this dispute. She was told that it 'wasn't the way things were done'. She felt that everyone had expectations of how she, as a low-paid, former NUPE member, should behave. By being outspoken, she felt that she had gone against these expectations.

Another example concerns the National Minimum Wage (NMW). The national minimum wage was a major issue pursued by UNISON in its early years (see Morris, 2000 and Thornley, 2000 for further details). As such, it is a topic that was pursued in a number of committees. It is useful to begin this discussion at the 1995 National Delegate Conference. Conference passed a composite motion on full employment, committing UNISON to campaign for a minimum wage of at least half median male earnings (at the time this equated to approximately £4.15). This motion was the basis of the UNISON motion submitted to the 1995 TUC, but the UNISON motion did not mention the specific figure of £4.15. When the NMW was debated in the afternoon session of the TUC on 13 September 1995, it was interrupted by a demonstration of women walking in front of the conference stage wearing white t-shirts with the figure £4.15 clearly printed on them in black. Watching the debate on television, I recognised many of the women as UNISON members whom I had met during my research. The TUC debate was widely reported in the press the next day, with one national newspaper reporting that UNISON had not been paying their own staff the recommended minimum wage.

Comparing the Regional Women's Committee meeting on the following day (14 September), and the response of the Regional Committee, a week later, best illustrate the different levels of awareness and interest in the national minimum wage. Information (provided by the regional TUC) about the NMW was introduced to the Regional Women's Committee by the Women's Officer who thought the Committee 'might want to think about promoting national minimum wage in the Region'. Reference was made to the newspaper allegation concerning UNISON staff not receiving the minimum wage. A key member of the Women's Committee defended UNISON and noted that the workplace was at the seaside, the staff were casual, and reference had to be taken of the geographical location. Another member of the committee noted that these remarks were 'contentious', noting, 'that's the whole point. It's £4.15 across the country.' However, when asked if the committee wanted to do anything about the NMW the committee decided to table it at the next meeting. This level of debate contrasts with a considerable debate on the NMW that took place at the mainstream Regional Committee on 25 September. In particular, members of the TUC delegation present on the Regional Committee were called to account for UNISON dropping the figure of £4.15 within one month of it being agreed at National Delegate Conference.

A member of the Regional Committee in Region 2 confirmed the political nature of the NMW debate within UNISON. She noted that the TUC demonstration came out of a lunch shared by a number of like-minded women, one of whom took the idea on through the organisation, Socialist Women on Male Platforms (SWOMP). The preparation for the exercise was carried out in secret and the men complained that they could not join in. Although many UNISON women were involved in the protest, the member insisted that it was independent of the lay delegation in UNISON. She noted that the issue was a political one, not an issue of the official/lay relationship. Because of the politics of being 'tied' to the official policy of the Labour Party, pressing the issue of £4.15 at the TUC was seen as 'rocking the boat'.

A new member of the Women's Committee noted that the Women's Committee appeared to be apolitical in its approach:

> I was looking forward to meeting women like myself. I thought it would be interesting to meet women from other service groups who are active in other ways. I thought I would learn a lot. I thought it would help in getting involved. I had expectations of the committee being political. I was expecting something radical, something about change, challenging the union itself from inside and challenging externally.

However, this is not to say that women in the women's structures were devoid of political awareness – it just took a different form. It is the case that women (and men) in the mainstream structures discussed gender inequality from a macro-economic perspective and discussed national measures for ameliorating the worst effects of women's low pay – views that were not discussed in the women's structures. However, women in the women's structures raised very specific workplace reasons for why women earned less money – none of which were raised or discussed in the mainstream structures.

Tables 9.1 and 9.2 illustrate the limited overlap between issues discussed in the mainstream and women-only committees. These tables have been compiled from mainstream debates and concerns raised by women at the Regional Women's Committee and two women-only educational events. Although it is the intention that the Regional Women's Forum sets the agenda for women's organisation in this Region, no Forum was held during the period of my research. Tables 9.1 and 9.2 show that few concerns that women identify as their concerns are discussed at Regional Committee and Regional Council. Likewise, a review of issues debated at Regional Committee and Regional Council indicates that few are discussed within the regional women's structures (McBride, 1997).

Women within the women's structures highlighted a number of ways in which they wanted to achieve equality at work. These included the provision of affordable childcare facilities, equal pay, job evaluation, promotion, and positive action training. The identification of these issues illustrates the difference between making gender differences visible on the mainstream committee and challenging male norms at a local level. For example, the cleaners' dispute illustrated the extent to which Regional Committee members were prepared to 'fight' for the rights of members, and highlight the rights of women members in particular. However, women in the women's structures tended to look at the processes of inequality rather than protest at the outcome. Job segregation and its implications for men and women were discussed in the women-only structures – not in the mainstream committees.

Reference has already been made to the Equal Opportunities Commission Report on Compulsory Competitive Tendering (CCT) (Escott and Whitfield, 1995). When this was discussed in the Women's Committee, the women talked about their need for more information about the issue and the need for more training. One member noted that 90 per cent of members who went on the CCT training courses in Local Government were male. Another member noted that training was not widespread and that since one male in her branch does all the negotiations, he had 'brushed off' the need for anyone else to be trained. The women did not dispute that lay officers (for example, branch secretaries and convenors) should be, and were being, trained in CCT and TUPE (Transfer of Undertakings (Protection of Employment) Regulations 1981). The women, however, added another perspective. They felt that unless rank-and-file members also had an understanding of CCT and

TUPE, they would not be fully equipped to engage meaningfully with any debates on the issue. Although earlier sections indicate that these women were not challenging political structures at a broader level (for example, through industrial activity and the NMW), such discussions indicated that they were not averse to challenging male norms at a local level.

Table 9.1   Internal issues of concern to women in Region 2

Discussed in women's structures/ activities	*Discussed in women's structures/ activities and Regional committee/ Council*
Constitution of women's structure National Women's Conference National Delegate Conference (NDC) Childcare expenses at NDC Women's education Organisation of women Fair representation of black women Direct mailings of women-only courses Childcare room in Congress House, TUC Updating mailing list system Training for local bargaining/CCT and TUPE	Timing of meetings Facilities time Time off for meetings (health, nightworkers) Proportionality at branch level Inaccurate membership records

    Caring responsibilities was another issue raised by women in the region but not heard within the mainstream regional structures. The regional structure provides an important means of highlighting this issue at a more localised level. It is branches that need to negotiate childcare facilities for workers and it is branch representatives who attend the Regional Council and Regional Committee. During the period of my research, one of the other regional Women's Committees published a substantial booklet on negotiating childcare for workers. There is considerable potential for discussing and circulating such a text through branch representatives attending the mainstream Regional Committees. However, at the time of my research, such options were not being explored. Detailed study within this region suggests that two factors support the limited discussion of women's concerns in mainstream committees.   The first relates to the institutional mechanisms of group representation in this region.   The second relates to the din of other issues.

Table 9.2   External issues of concern to women in Region 2

Discussed in women's structures/ activities	*Discussed in women's structures/ activities and Regional Committee/ Council*
New employee rights for part-time workers	National Minimum Wage
Sexual harassment	Boycott of employer in dispute
Gender implications of CCT	Support for strike action
Maternity/paternity leave	Pensions
Difficulties of childcare for shiftworkers	
Impact of multi-skilling on women	
Job segregation	
Job evaluation/ study of wage differentials	
Equal pay	
Promotion	
Positive action training	
Sickness policies	
Breast cancer-screening scheme	
Nestlé Boycott	
Changes in divorce law	
Labour Party: Governing for Democracy	
Attendance at demonstrations/rallies	
Domestic violence	
Contraception	
Full employment	

Limitations on group representation

As noted in Chapter 3, UNISON's rule book provides resources for women's self-organised groups to meet together, establish their own priorities and have group representation in regional structures. Also, as argued in Chapter 3, although this generates new forms of authority and influence for women, the rule book does not provide women as a group with adequate power in relation to privileged groups. Decision makers are not obliged to take account of policies generated by women as a group and women are not provided with veto power regarding policies that affect them directly. The perception of the Women's Officer in Region 2, and others in the wider union, was that women's self-organisation had no power in UNISON. The solution of Region 2 was to organise women shop stewards and train them to 'run the union'. However, this was a long-term strategy that would take a long time to develop. In the meantime, there was a need to organise strategically at regional level.

Chapters 5 and 7 provided evidence of self-organised groups working together at regional level to gain collective authority and influence. I saw very little of this activity in Region 2. Indeed, the women's structure in Region 2 was criticised by the Lesbian and Gay members' Self-organised Group for leaving out 'the member'. Although a few women were on both committees, a number of women on the mainstream regional committee had their concerns about the legitimate role of the women's structures. I interviewed seven women who sat on the Regional Committee and six of these women expressed their concerns about women's self-organsiation. Extracts from three of these interviews are noted below:

> Self-organisation cuts across proportionality – in terms of what self-organised women and women activists want – and it creates tension and conflict ... Who do the self-organised women speak for? ... their democratic accountability is suspect and they are not necessarily mandated.

> There is a danger of self-organisation not representing everyone. It's missing working class women ... Self-organisation is a self-indulgent wank.

> On balance it is better to have self-organisation for women but how it operates is problematic. It is open to abuse on grounds of accountability and take over by factions because the oppressed are not open to challenge.

Without coercive power and few alliances, the representative of the Regional Women's Committee has limited facilities with which to win arguments expressed on behalf of women in the women's structures. In addition, the regional structure in Region 2 was likely to exacerbate this position. Reference was made in Chapter 2 to Phillips' (1991, 1993) arguments against group representation of women. She argued that there were few mechanisms for enabling women's voices to be heard or women's perspectives to be agreed. Although the women's structure in Region 2 enabled the voices of women shop stewards to be heard, it had omitted a policy-making forum at regional level in which policy could be decided and represented at the mainstream Regional Committee. Attention to providing institutional mechanisms to collect and represent women's concerns was most important, given the mobilisation of bias towards the discussion of other issues.

The din of other issues

As noted above, the region's function is to operate in an intermediary role between branches and the national level and across service groups. Observation of the Regional Committee and Council over the period of a year showed that activity tended to be focused on three underlying issues – each of which took up considerable debating time and energy. The first related to external issues of industrial action against job cuts and hostile employers, the latter two related to internal issues of union democracy.

An analysis of interview material and election addresses of successful candidates provides more information about individual expectations of the regional role and shows the expectations of the committee being an active body within the region that 'fights' for jobs, and 'defends' job cuts. The desire to make a difference in the lives of working people within the region resonates through the addresses:

> The defence of jobs and services in all industries in which UNISON organises must be top of the Region's agenda. (Regional Committee member, 1995 election address)

> The region must continue to campaign in all sectors, fighting job cuts whether they be in the Gas or the Health Service, giving members the ability to determine their future. (Regional Committee member, 1995 election address)

> I want to see [Region 2] taking a lead within UNISON on fighting cuts and job losses, in defending services and preventing closures ... I am standing for re-election to keep on pushing on the Regional Committee for UNISON to stop pretending it's a legal aid or friendly society and to start acting like a trade union. (Regional Committee member, election address)

However, these intentions tended to be thwarted by the regional structure. The Regional Committee cannot deal with specific service group issues, since this is the responsibility of regional service groups. For example, motions concerning the defence of national terms and conditions in a Local Government branch and the motion from a Health Service branch regarding the abolition of Regional Health Authorities were ruled out of order because they were deemed the remit of the regional service groups.

Most issues related to internal issues of union structures and practices. Given the relatively young age of UNISON during my period of research, perhaps it was inevitable that the Regional Committee spent considerable time discussing constitutions and internal issues of democracy. Indeed, considerably more time was spent discussing external issues in the later meetings I attended. However, it is likely that internal issues are likely to occupy considerable discussion time in the future too. This is because the region represents a key focal point at which to pursue two unresolved issues noted in Chapter 3 above (Fryer, 2000), the first being the relationship between paid officers and lay representatives. The second issue was the relationship between regions and the centre. A senior lay activist explained:

> The fundamental dynamic within the union (at any level) is protecting lay members' access and preventing the erosion of key principles by full-time officers – which everybody sees as a threat. Not everybody agrees what is a threat, and all define lay members in different ways. For members of Campaign for a Fighting Democratic Unison (CFDU), lay members are the rank and file (i.e. not members of the NEC). Whereas ex-NUPE members may come to the same conclusion, but on a different platform.

A number of political groupings existed in Region 2 to take these issues further. CFDU was suitably well organised within UNISON to put forward their candidate in the election for General Secretary. Amongst other things, the candidate stood for 'genuine lay member control of UNISON, as opposed to domination by non-elected full-time officials'. A member of the Regional Committee noted there was a 'handful of major committed activists who had longer-term activity with the Labour Party, the Communist Party, or the "Trots'". However, another member of the Regional Committee noted the fluidity of these groupings

> Alliances across former partner union lines are natural since people know each other. There is quite a strong alliance around 'Fighting for a Democratic Union' which is quite successful. There are also strong ties around service groups – particularly health. But there are different groupings at different times. It is too simplistic to say that the same competing agendas always operate.

Considerable time was spent discussing democratic structures and practices within Regional Committee and Regional Council and it could be argued that they were raised to the exclusion of external issues, and women's concerns. Two experienced women activists on the Committee identified the implication of strong political views for the discussion of women's concerns:

> I worry about political factionalism. It has the potential to cut out issues of importance and is very hard to do anything about. We need to provide opportunities to meet across factions.

> Women's issues are wide ranging and political groupings are stronger and take precedence with issues still being analysed from a political perspective.

This was also a concern of the Women's Committee representative who noted 'Some women are more interested in political activity rather than UNISON's activity and I am concerned that women wanting to push ahead are being blocked.'

Motions submitted to the Council were from a wider, political perspective, and mostly relate to internal issues, international matters, state policy, Labour Party policy, or national trade union movement issues. Few issues relate specifically to employment issues, because to be ruled in, they need to be relevant to all service groups. A member of the Regional Committee and Women's Committee told me how she had addressed a Regional Council meeting, saying that she was appalled by the discussions and their lack of relevance to her members. This analysis was reiterated by the observation of a Regional Officer:

> It's difficult to persuade members to attend – they don't feel it is relevant
> and feel that they have to put up with being talked down if they want to
> make a point. It is not seen as a priority when they have much lower
> facilities time.

At a time when branch officers are grappling with local issues of
contracting out and redundancies, it may be too much to expect delegates
to attend a Council meeting which discusses issues – albeit worthy – that
appear tangential to their main concerns.   Added to this was the
possibility that they might make the effort to attend and the meeting could
be inquorate. A recent survey of attendance had noted that approximately
eighty branches were not registering to attend the Council and only 40 per
cent of those that had registered were attending. Branches not attending
were mostly small health branches. A key (female) activist noted 'It is
difficult to find out what the problem is - probably because there is no one
single answer. It probably relates to relationships to fellow workers, own
workload and individuals making decisions not to attend.'

Three other women endorsed these comments. One noted that 'as a
member in the frontline, I'm fighting against my own conscience to
attend.' Another agreed that the 'workplace situation makes it difficult',
and a third noted that she felt 'uncomfortable with colleagues when going
to meetings'.

Low attendance at Regional Council had a dramatic effect on
democratic processes within the Region. Figures from the Region's first
AGM reveal the deficit of delegates. Out of 425 delegates, 176 delegates
registered to attend the AGM. Of these 176, 130 actually attended. I
attended four Regional Council meetings in Region 2 over a period of a
year. One meeting did not start because it was not quorate and another
two were prematurely closed when they became inquorate after lunch.
This undermined the role of the Regional Committee. Within Region 2,
the Regional Council was frequently reminded that it was the decision
maker for the region, thus ensuring that the Regional Committee was in
effect only the management committee for the region. That is, the
Committee was there to carry out the wishes of the Council rather than to
act on its own. However, the tendency for the Regional Council to be
inquorate meant that, in practice, policy decisions were not made on a
frequent basis. In this hierarchical structure, the expectations of members
of the Committee could be undermined by the failure of the Council. One
member noted how the Council could be manipulated to fail:

I believe some members and officers are openly hostile to Council and that some officers see it as a waste of time. Some parties are gleeful when it is inquorate. Branches are not encouraged to attend, or change their behaviour and attend. A few would like to see it die a death.

The number of members exceeding the quorum was very low at the first meeting I attended and it was possible to see the contribution which non-attendees made to the democratic process. After lunch, the meeting needed two counts to ensure that it was still quorate. After the Council had heard a guest speaker and a contentious motion had been discussed (and carried), a number of people left the hall. During the moving of the next motion, someone called the meeting 'inquorate', and on finding that a quorum was not present, the meeting was promptly closed. Given that a number of speakers for and against the motion had invoked calls for democracy within the union, it was quite ironic that by leaving the room after it had been discussed, some of the same speakers (exercising their democratic right) were able to immediately disenfranchise the rest of the meeting. One member (also a member of the Women's Committee) argued that members were using 'waffle' to manipulate decisions in several ways:

Democracy is being manipulated [at the Region Council]. Certain groups nit-pick issues at the council meetings, then people leave and whatever the politicking group want, they push in to get it through. I don't like Friday or Monday Council meetings. Time-off is granted for all day. Some people make a long weekend of it and by Friday afternoon, the meeting may be inquorate. Knowing that the meeting may be inquorate in the afternoon, some parties may waffle on about issues, so that other motions are not discussed ... Women don't tend to do this as they are up front. I wonder whether they should do, and fight fire with fire, get better organised, and get more women involved.

Notwithstanding the latter comment, it was a woman who had called the meeting inquorate, and had done so for her own reasons. She said that she had called the meeting inquorate 'To stop the "Trots" controlling the meeting, and before the Regional Council were asked to back up the motion with money.'

By focusing on the processes of democracy and defining democracy in terms of the lay–paid officer relationship, arguably less time was spent discussing wider issues and making policy. Furthermore, the representative structures appeared to exacerbate this tendency.

Representative structures

In all meetings of the Regional Committee, the Agenda was essentially a framework for feedback: matters arising from previous Minutes, report back from NEC members and TUC representatives, report-back from sub-committees of the Committee, the Regional Secretary's Report and the Financial Report. Most meetings, therefore, had a tendency to be reactive and inward looking, with limited proactive activity. External issues were seldom discussed, and when they were, they were usually the subject of motions to or from Regional Council, or were raised under 'Any Other Business'. Although I have attributed this to the business of the Agenda, it is obviously drawn up by someone and, as noted in Chapter 2 above, agendas are vulnerable to manipulation and bias. However, having sat on a number of different UNISON committees during the period of my research, the Agendas of this Committee seemed little different to the Agendas of any of the other committees – including the Women's Committees. So, in part, feedback-driven Agendas are a symptom of representative structures of democracy. If a committee has sent a representative to another meeting, or a conference, it needs to know what that representative did. Likewise a committee will want to know what a working group has achieved. Thus, of a finite period of time, a considerable amount is taken up by feedback reports. If members wish to protest about an issue not on the Agenda, they raise it in Matters Arising (from previous Minutes), or Any Other Business. Indeed, considerable time was spent on 'Matters Arising' during the committees observed during my research. The more time that is spent hearing feedback and discussing internal democracy, the less time there is to discuss external, proactive issues. This perpetuated the very phenomena that individuals and groups were often fighting against. Due to lack of time, matters requiring detailed thought and discussion were often left to the next meeting, or the 'management team' (consisting of key lay and paid officers).

Many members realised the important relationship between time and membership control and often demanded more time in terms of more meetings, or longer meetings. However, these demands ignore the concerns of those having difficulty taking time off for meetings. Often, these members were members in the Health Care Service Group, and invariably women. Reference was made in Chapter 4 to the Regional Health Committee in Region 2 wanting direct elections for the Regional Committee, because insufficient health service members were able to come to the Regional Council to vote. That meeting was reminded that members in health care 'don't have time off'. When the Women's Committee discussed the timing of meetings, they noted the difficulty of getting time-off facilities for night-workers. The issue of time off was discussed at a meeting of the Regional Committee and prompted an interesting debate in terms of member participation. Of the 16 recorded comments, men made four, and there was a high degree of consensus amongst the women who were talking. This was one issue where women were in agreement.

Reference was made in Chapter 2 to the differentiated access that women had to resources and facility time at work. If we add to this the difficulty of getting time off in health, and the possibility of needing to make provision for domestic responsibilities during meeting times, then women's access to decision-making arenas may be seriously undermined. This could be further exacerbated by the needs of a representative structure where key activity and decision making is the remit of sub-committees and working group. Reference was made in Chapter 4 to the power of different sub-committees in national Service Groups, and it seems that similar observations could be made at a regional level. Frequently, although the Regional Committee was the ultimate arbiter of decisions, it was reacting to the outcome of debates which had already taken place elsewhere. Thus, if one were looking to influence activity and debates in the region, sub-committees of the Regional Committee would appear to be a good place to start. Women on the Regional Women's Committee had obviously appreciated this and had stood for election to the Recruitment and Organisation sub-committee. From here they attempted to ensure that proportionality and fair representation were implemented at branch level, and monitoring was part of the Agenda. However, it is difficult to reconcile the need to sit on a number of committees in order to 'make a difference', and the difficulties which many members have in getting time off for meetings. Whilst discussions of democracy are centred on the lay–officer relationship, it is unlikely that more innovative discussions about enabling more members to participate will evolve. A key (female) activist of the Regional Committee asked:

How can you radically reconstruct that which people are actively involved in? Within my own branch, I wanted to get less branch executive meetings, and more department support meetings, but I was accused of Stalinism, and a lack of democracy. How do you move forward in such circumstances?

Summary and discussion

The study of mainstream and women-only structures in Region 2 enabled a number of questions to be addressed. Proportionality and fair representation facilitated the election of women to the Regional Committee in proportion to their membership within the region. As well as gaining access to the decision-making forum, women contributed to all debates, thus ensuring that 'natural justice' was attained in terms of women's participation. However, it did not mean that all women were speaking, or that women's concerns were debated on a regular basis within the mainstream structures.

For women to gain full access to decision-making processes within mainstream structures they needed to be able to attend the meeting and they needed to speak. In relation to the Regional Council, sufficient numbers of their colleagues had to be present for the meeting to be quorate. Finally, women needed to know the rules of the game and be prepared to use them. Not all women were willing or able to do this. Some members were unable to attend meetings due to work commitments. Newly active women did not tend to speak at meetings and a number of the Regional Council meetings were inquorate.

Although present at the meetings, women were under no obligation to talk for women. The interest of many candidates was to ensure that the union at regional level was a campaigning organisation – to defend jobs and services. Only one woman on the Regional Committee has a legitimate mandate to speak for 'women in the region', and this is the representative of the Women's Committee. This chapter illustrates that the Women's Committee pursues a different role within UNISON to that of the Regional Committee. Whilst members would like to see the Regional Committee as the co-ordinator of campaigns, the role of the Women's Committee was primarily focused on women's organisation and education. Thus, at the time of the study, the priorities and concerns of the Women's Committee were different to those of the Regional Committee. With one or two exceptions, issues raised in the Regional

Committee were not the subject of debate at the Women's Committee, and issues raised in the Women's Committee were not the subject of debate at the Regional Committee (or Council). Whilst a representative of the Women's Committee gained access to the Regional Committee, the Women's Committee was not using this access to pursue specific issues on a systematic basis (although it had evidently done so in the past). Nor had it started to nominate other women to the Regional Committee. At the time of writing, therefore, it was not acting as a pressure group, or as a conduit for 'like-minded' women to access the Regional Committee. It was, however, working with women shop stewards at a branch level and encouraging women to participate at their workplace. Since most issues discussed at the Regional Committee are raised through branches, and nominations to Regional Council and Regional Committee are from branches, such activity could see the beginning of a changing agenda – but such a strategy will take time to bear fruit.

I would argue, however, that more than time is required before a change of agenda. Whilst this branch-based strategy supports the increased involvement of newly active women who are more likely to raise gendered workplace concerns, it neglects the fact that a considerable number of experienced women are already involved in the mainstream committees. It is not possible to argue that the 'previously active' women do not identify with women, or do not represent women's concerns. Instead, it would appear that previously active women analyse women's concerns from a political perspective, rather than a gendered perspective. Members in the women's structure are keen to talk about job segregation, but not so keen to talk about the national minimum wage. Women in the mainstream structures are keen to talk about national political solutions, but do not talk about changing women's segregation at a local level. As noted in Chapters 2 and 3, both perspectives are needed. Indeed, the work of Higgins (1996) suggests that women's concerns will go unheard whilst unions persist with a gender-neutral perspective. Within UNISON, the danger is that the two perspectives never meet on equal terms, or neutral territory. Both sets of women invest their time in structures that seldom interact.

That democracy continues to be analysed predominantly in terms of the lay–paid officer relationship has implications for the effective representation of women, and their concerns. This analysis of democracy does not connect with the feminist analysis of democracy and does not perceive that the 'work' of participation, is different for different peoples.

This model of democracy sets the agenda of debate at committee meetings and is in danger of occupying precious debating time to the exclusion of workplace-based discussions. Furthermore, by defining democracy through the lay–paid officer relationship, committee members focus on gender-neutral outcomes for members, but they seldom look at democracy in terms of outcomes for women.

10 The Reshaping of Democracy?

This book has studied the pursuit of gender democracy in UNISON. Gender democracy was defined in Chapter 1 as a system in which there is equality between men and women. This concept was used because the word 'democracy' implies equality even though it does not necessarily mean democracy will be or has been achieved. In its commitment to proportionality, fair representation and self-organisation, UNISON's rule book explicitly provides for gender democracy. However, as indicated in Chapter 2, democracy is shaped by pulls towards ideals and prescriptions and resistance from the reality of what already exists (Sartori, 1965, 1987). The reality of democracy includes predominant values that operate to the benefit of certain groups at the expense of others (Bachrach and Barataz, 1970). A number of trade union studies have shown how predominant values have operated to benefit men and privilege them as a specific membership group. The extent to which unions can change these values and support a broader membership has implications for the future size and shape of unions.

The first part of this chapter addresses two questions raised by Bachrach and Baratz (1970): how are new sources of power generated, and how do these new sources of power alter political processes and lessen inequality of representation between members? The implementation of UNISON's three rule-book commitments to gender democracy are reviewed and the one- and two-dimensional views of power are used to indicate how the ideals of the rule book are turned into reality. The second part of the chapter returns to the prescriptions for gender democracy derived from the literature and indicates the implications of this study for past and future work. The chapter concludes with three key issues that emerge from UNISON's radical attempts to pursue gender democracy.

The generation of new sources of power

Proportionality and fair representation

Feminist studies of trade union democracy have shown how elections have tended to favour the interests of privileged groups. Chapters 3, 4 and 6 show how it is possible to implement proportionality and fair representation so as to limit the election of representatives from privileged groups and facilitate the election of representatives from oppressed social groups. Both principles required a preparedness to identify specific groups of constituents and facilitate mirror representation by either pre- or post-categorisation of seats according to sex, economic status and race. They required multi-representative constituencies and were supported by the capacity to rerun elections for vacant seats.

Multi-representative constituencies are a key feature of the rule book-defined National Executive Council (NEC). However, this characteristic needed to be negotiated on other committees. Analysis of these negotiations provided some indication of the level of resistance to change. Direct conflict was one indicator. Non-decision making was another (Bachrach and Baratz, 1970). Chapter 4 illustrated how officers tended to limit the use of multi-representative constituencies and activists (albeit not always immediately) tended to expand their use. Although earlier studies of women in trade unions have provided vivid accounts of men maintaining their representative power, this study provided a mixed picture of male-based resistance.

Although officers, mostly male, mobilised bias against the expansion of a key characteristic of proportionality (that is, multi-representative constitutions), male activists did not generally support these arguments. On the contrary, arguments against multi-representative constituencies have often been rejected and overturned by male and female activists working together. The study would suggest that some men already favoured by the 'rules of the game' see the participation and representation of women as an opportunity for more power rather than a challenge to their existing power. This can be seen in Chapter 5, which identifies how existing groups push and pull women into standing for electoral positions.

This is not to say that male resistance does not exist. The conflict surrounding low-paid seats on the Health Care Service Group Executive

(HCSGE) and the woman accused of blocking a 'general' NEC seat are examples of male-based resistance. They suggest that male-based resistance is more likely when men believe that women's representation will be at the expense of their own representation. This study also raises the questions about the gender bias of officers. The paid-officer group in UNISON is male-dominated and the mobilisation of bias against increasing lay representation did have implications for gender democracy.

This mixed picture illustrates the cross-cutting and fluid nature of oppressed social groups (Young, 1990). Although women are an oppressed social group in relation to men, this does not preclude individual women being members of a privileged group, in relation to oppressed social groups of working-class, or black members. Likewise, whilst male manual workers were members of the privileged group of men in former NUPE and COHSE, they could be construed as members of the oppressed social group of working-class members within UNISON. What is the most appropriate interpretation of the mobilisation of bias towards former partner unions being a component of fair representation? From one angle this could be interpreted as male-based resistance from male manual members who are being replaced by manual women members. From another perspective it could be interpreted as resistance to a perceived mobilisation of bias to the benefit of middle-class, white-collar members. More generally, such issues raise important questions about the appropriate balance to be made between the reservation of seats for individuals of oppressed social groups.

This section has dealt primarily with gender-based resistance to proportionality and fair representation. Conflict and non-decision making concerning the representation of black, lesbian and gay, and disabled members also shaped democratic processes. The rule book was initially silent on the issue of representation by individuals of other oppressed social groups. This silence, and resistance to change illustrates that there are boundaries to the willingness of activists to increase representation of oppressed social groups. The rule book has been changed to allow regional self-organised groups to nominate candidates for the NEC and self-organised groups gained representation at service group conferences. However, I think it is important to note that these changes were achieved by increasing the total number of representatives. The test of whether privileged groups identify the interests of oppressed social groups as their own will be their acceptance of greater diversity amongst a fixed number of seats.

Self-organisation

A recent survey of trade union structures illustrates the extent to which the use of women-only structures is an accepted institutional practice, or norm, within trade unions (Southern and Eastern Regional TUC Women's Rights Committee, 2000). This case study has illustrated the extent to which UNISON is prepared to support self-organisation and, in turn, how women's self-organisation has supported collective empowerment and reflection. Women have used self-organisation in UNISON to talk about things that were not normally discussed at branch-level union meetings. They discussed pensions, domestic violence, harassment, work-related stress and personal development. In common with other studies, women in UNISON found these women-only events extremely supportive and comfortable and often used this space to participate in union activity for the first time. They also used these spaces to learn more about the union, and how it operated. Networks of interested women developed at regional level and regional women's newsletters were being used to get relevant information to as many other women as possible. The latter was deemed particularly useful for circumventing any branch 'gatekeepers' who were not interested in encouraging women to the same extent.

However, despite the very strong pull of these prescriptions, the study of self-organisation in Regions 1 and 2 suggests that these prescriptions were resisted along at least two dimensions. First, the nature and role of self-organisation itself was challenged by some of the women operating in the women-only structures. Second, men as a group were accused of resisting the establishment of self-organised groups at branch level. Although there are distinct differences between these sources of resistance, it is likely that, together, they made up the broad section of the National Delegate Conference that was resistant to the consolidation of influence and resources of the National Women's Conference.

Resistance to self-organisation is not unusual. What is different in this study is the attempt by the women's group in Region 2 to use the framework of women's self-organisation to organise women shop stewards. Whilst some might dismiss this resistance as deriving from women who had little tradition of self-organisation within their former partner unions, a consideration of the responses to group representation would seem to confirm their critical assessment of the ambiguity and powerlessness of self-organisation within UNISON.

Group representation

As noted in Chapter 3, self-organised groups have rights of representation at regional level. This challenges the dominant norm that representatives are elected by all the constituents in the particular constituency, rather than a sub-set of constituents. This was a rule-book commitment which was extended in Region 1. Self-organised groups in this region proposed to double the number of representatives from each group to the Regional Council from one to two. This was accepted without conflict. However, as noted earlier, regional structures are general committees and do not relate to collective bargaining agendas. The more important dynamic related to responses to the extension of group representation to service group structures.

The Lesbian and Gay Members Self-organised Group proposed an extension of representation to all service group structures. This was resisted at most levels but access to the national conference was accepted. Bachrach and Baratz (1970) note that certain contests are 'lost' because the apparent losers consider the issues inconsequential. It could be argued that this group representation was accepted because providing seats for two (non-voting) representatives from each self-organised group was unlikely to challenge dominant values.

As noted in Chapter 2, the institutional mechanisms advocated by Young (1990) and Cockburn (1996) provide oppressed social groups with the ability to win arguments through the use of coercive power. Although use of the word 'coercive' implies an aggressive form of power, it arguably provides oppressed social groups with more negotiating capacity than that which can be obtained through increasing the number of individual representatives from oppressed social groups. Although UNISON has taken tentative steps to give representation rights to oppressed social groups, this has not dramatically increased their power in relation to privileged groups.

The powerlessness of oppressed social groups

This study has noted that self-organised groups do not automatically have rights of access to a number of committees within UNISON. The case studies of the women's groups suggest that there is a preferred model for self-organised groups within UNISON. The common oppression of members in self-organised groups is recognised by mainstream committees inasmuch as self-organised groups are able to organise themselves in their own way so that they may determine their own interests in isolation from the elements that might oppress them. However, when it comes to a consideration of their interests, self-organised groups are deemed to have equal power to any other organised group of members within the union. They do not have the power of veto over any decisions that might disproportionately affect members of their group. They have no automatic right of access to service-specific decision-making arenas within the union.

The predominant model of self-organisation within UNISON is of a pressure group whose comments are welcome but not necessarily taken into consideration. In essence, although much has been implemented within UNISON, the longest agenda of equal opportunities, that advocates representation by individuals of oppressed social groups *and* representation of oppressed social groups has not been fully implemented. Although UNISON's structure facilitates the representation of individual women and provides considerable support to women's self-organisation, it has not significantly increased the power of women as an oppressed social group.

Within the current structure, identity groups have union resources with which to participate but they have little power if they are not involved in the representative structures. This outcome can be contrasted with well-organised interest groups that may have no union resources, but achieve power through the mobilisation of their members within the representative structures. Interest groups expertly use the rules to engage fully in the game of representative democracy. Whilst the women-only groups may be discussing women's concerns, they are without power to take them forward unless they have representative links in the mainstream committees. Members in the mainstream committees feel that this is a legitimate stance given the voluntary nature of membership in identity groups. It may also reflect the practical implications of giving representative rights to all four of the self-organised groups, rather than solely to women. It does, however, leave self-organised groups reliant on individual representatives or effective alliances with other groups.

The reliance on individual women to push women's concerns is a limited strategy. Although women representatives do speak for women, there are several reasons why women are not likely to speak for women on a systematic and regular basis. The first derives from their election from a mixed constituency, the second from their loyalties to sub-constituencies. Alliances between privileged and oppressed social groups, and amongst oppressed social groups, do provide valuable sources of power, but may not provide an acceptable long-term strategy for power. Members, activists and political groups have mobilised around employer-based disputes and women, as a group, have arguably gained coercive power through these alliances. However, although political groups have supported women fighting job and pay cuts, it remains to be seen whether women, as a group, support the longer-term objectives of these political groups. Prescriptions for empowering oppressed social groups through group representation are controversial but I believe are worthy of debate. They require two elements – a preparedness to provide representative seats on all committees for oppressed social groups and a preparedness to take account of group views.

This chapter has discussed the manner in which the rule book ideals and reality of gender democracy interfered and collided with each other and described the structural outcomes. The chapter now returns to the original prescriptions for gender democracy – as derived from the literature – and notes the implications of this study for the evolution of gender democracy.

Gender democracy: an evolving model

Prescriptions to address exclusion through domestic commitments

This study reiterates that family-friendly practices, such as the provision of crèche facilities and childcare allowances, are an important part of women's participation in the union. Although these facilities tackle symptoms they do not tackle causes and, at the time of this research, there was no strategy to tackle the unequal distribution of responsibilities in the household. Power relations in the home, however, were being discussed in relation to domestic violence. Monies were being donated, radical motions were written and booklets on domestic violence were being circulated to branches.

The study also confirmed the importance of facilities agreements to female union activism (Lawrence, 1994). Lawrence's case study of a former NALGO local government branch indicated that trade union facilities agreements were one of two factors that promoted women's participation and representation.   Although I was not studying union activities at branch level, the importance of time off for union activities was frequently mentioned by activists – in relation to their own attendance at meetings and the activity of their colleagues at all levels of the union.   This is a particularly important issue for the continued representation of low-paid and part-time women workers.   Reference was made in Chapter 6 to the number of vacant low-paid women's seats and I note that it remains an issue for more recent elections held in 2000.   The existence of these vacant seats cannot be divorced from the lived experiences of low paid and part-time women described in Chapter 8. Although UNISON has done much to provide structural support for the representation of low-paid women, these seats are likely to remain vacant until the processes of representation take more account of these experiences.

Prescriptions for paid officers

Reference has already been made to resistance from paid officers, mostly male, to certain aspects of gender democracy.   This reiterates the need to recruit more women officers and emphasises the importance of UNISON's Women's Development Project (UNISON, 1998b; Wheeler, 2000).   Another prescription concerned the need to discourage sexist behaviour and provide a harassment-free working environment.   During this study, activists raised concerns about the procedure for investigating allegations of harassment of paid officers. Activists organised around this issue in UNISON and a new policy was written into the rule book.   The policy indicates that UNISON employees have the right not to be harassed by UNISON members and sets down the investigation procedure for investigating allegations.

The implications of this study for debates about the centralisation of power are less easy to establish.   Kelly and Heery (1994) argued that a centralisation of power could enable the conservation, mobilisation and targeting of resources on priority issues such as membership recruitment and campaigns over women's rights.   In the merger negotiations, NUPE and COHSE argued for the joint determination of future strategy by senior paid officers and national lay representatives (Fryer, 2000). However, as noted in Chapter 3, the connection between this strategy and the pursuit of equal opportunities does not appear to have been made, nor was it made during debates about the level of money to be retained by branches. Debates concerning the lay–officer relationship continued to be gender-neutral, were couched in terms of 'who runs this union?' and took a considerable amount of committee time. Indeed, the desire for joint determination, or partnership, appeared to have an adverse effect on the pursuit of equal opportunities when it underpinned lengthy competitive debates between members and paid officers and amongst different activist groups. In this respect, competition between activists did appear to be a pervasive feature of democracy (James, 1984). Overall, a mixed picture emerged of the relationship between national and regional paid officers and the pursuit of gender democracy. On the one hand, some male officers appeared to be blocking the generation of new sources of power for women. On the other hand, at times women officers were the only source of a gendered analysis of work. I am unable to throw much light on the centralisation thesis from the perspective of the branch, but a recent case study of two UNISON Local Government branches suggests the need for the 'simultaneous development of centralisation and decentralisation with closer articulation' (Park, 1999, p. 271) (see also Conley, 2000).

Prescriptions for representative democracy

This study has shown how the identification of women as individuals in a sex category supports the systematic inclusion of women in representative structures. It has also shown how the identification of members by economic income and race can support the inclusion of low-paid women and black members in representative structures. In UNISON, the priority has been to achieve fair representation of women. This has meant that divisions on the basis of economic class and race have tended to be pursued through women's seats. This has arguably led to the exclusion of male manual workers and black men and highlights the importance of achieving diversity across men, as well as women. This study has also provided information about two other aspects of representation – both of which have consequences for the representation of women by individual women. The first relates to the 'work' of representation, the second to the multiple interests of representatives.

This study has illustrated how proportionality has pushed and pulled newly active women into political processes that have not stood still while they learnt the 'rules'. If new institutional mechanisms are pulling in newly active members, unions need to recognise that – irrespective of gender – the skills of being a representative need to be learned. Representatives are subject to conflict, mobilisation of bias and suppression of interests and all members need to learn how to be effective representatives. Phillips talks of meetings being monopolised by those 'already favoured with wealth, education and power' (1991, p. 128). This study shows the need to add 'previous experience' and 'expertise' to that list. The newly active are less likely to speak and, as a result, the experienced become the shapers. This can have a detrimental effect on the discussion of workplace and gender issues.

The manner in which experienced members responded to the discussion of workplace issues gave me the impression that specific workplace issues are considered parochial and their discussion is seen as a feature of being 'newly active'. Hyman (1989) indicates that the detachment of decision making from members' experiences is part of a social relation that he calls 'bureaucracy'. It is possible to see this social process happening in mainstream regional and national meetings. The definition of 'union business' appeared to be wrapped up with notions of experience and ability to see the wider picture and excluded the discussion of workplace issues at national meetings. Earlier studies and debates illustrate that the bureaucratisation of representatives is not a gendered phenomenon, but it does have a gendered outcome. Although the process is the same for everyone, it has adverse implications for women because they are being distanced from discussing the very issues that are the basis of their subordination at work, for example, job segregation. Bureaucratisation is a double-blow for women because it distances them from the institutions that need to be changed. Whilst newly active women are more likely to discuss workplace issues, the theory of bureaucratisation implies that they too will soon adopt the predominant model of appropriate debate and stop talking about workplace issues. Hyman (1989) argues that unions need to organise in relation to workers' lived experiences but notes that this change must be membership initiated. Some of the work in this study suggests that women's groups may be a key to resolving that tension.

Women-only groups may have a powerful role in linking participatory and representative democracy. Pateman (1970) argues that participation at a local level provides practice in 'democratic skills and procedures'. The women-only group in Region 2 believed it was training women to 'run the union' through women-only education groups. The benefit of learning such skills in a women-only environment is that 'expertise' and 'democratic skills' could be conceptualised in a manner that is useful, rather than prohibitive, to women. The skills learnt in such groups could provide the means to challenge the bureaucratisation process that occurs within committees.

Other strategies that were used in the union were smaller working groups and caucus meetings. A more controversial strategy would be creating an awareness of patterns of participation. Stopping representatives from talking is anathema to most activists, but over-participation could be just as undemocratic as over-representation. If the systematic inclusion of women representatives has been achieved through the systematic exclusion of men, then the corollary about decision making is that men (and some women) need to be excluded from over-participating. Whilst this appears anti-democratic this is only what a number of the (mostly newly active) women have been doing. They have been excluding themselves from talking because they believe there is nothing to add to what has been said before, or because the debate is not seen as relevant.

A second aspect of representation indicated by this study relates to representativeness. Cockburn (1996) argues that women elected from a mixed constituency are not obliged to speak for their sex. Although the validity of this argument can be questioned in a female-dominated union, this study reveals a number of additional implications of representing a mixed-sex constituency. The literature cautions us against universalising the interests of all women and acknowledges the multiplicity of women's interests and concerns. However, there is an implicit assumption that this 'multiplicity of interests' reflects the opinions of women as a group. This study has shown that a single woman can often have a 'multiplicity of interests' which they choose to represent at different times.

A woman representative might speak simultaneously, or separately, for a geographical region, for an occupational group, for a political party, for women in general or for low-paid women, lesbian women, disabled women or black women in particular. Whilst this phenomenon is not specific to women, it needs to be built into the conceptualisation of women's concerns. It is important to realise that whilst women may share some common lived experiences concerning their subordinate position within society, they may chose not to prioritise these concerns all the time, or at any time. Whether women representatives speak for women is contingent on a number of factors, which is why it is important that the identification of women for the purposes of representative democracy is not the only mechanism for supporting women and other oppressed social groups.   It also has implications for self-organisation and group representation.

Prescriptions for self-organisation and group representation

The study showed that it is possible to develop self-organisation at the same time as supporting representative mechanisms such as proportionality.   It also showed that it is possible to pursue the representation of women as a sex category of individuals at the same time as representing women as an oppressed social group. This study has also illustrated the complexity of pursuing both strategies in tandem and highlighted the difference between self-organisation and group representation. More specifically it has indicated the problematic nature of representativeness as it relates to women as a social group. Reference has already been made to the multiplicity of interests within individual women and women as a group.   Indeed, although Young (1990) recognises that oppressed social groups are defined through a common history of oppression, she recognises the cross-cutting and fluid nature of the same groups. Cockburn (1996) recognises this issue too and seeks to resolve such issues with prescriptions for internal democracy in women's structures (p. 93) and effective alliances amongst women identified as individuals in a sex category and members of an oppressed social group (p. 94). This study confirms the importance of these prescriptions. If women as an oppressed social group are to gain rights of representation, then aggregating the multiplicity of interests amongst women is of paramount importance.   Without such mechanisms, 'which women represent women?' will continue to be asked. At the time of this study, in the words of one interviewee, women's self-organised groups were more likely to 'protect' rather than to 'project'. Later research by Colgan and Ledwith (2000) suggests that alliances amongst self-organised groups are the next stage in their development.

One aspect of internal democracy that led to a reconceptualisation of women's self-organisation was the desire of Region 2 to organise women shop stewards at branch level. For most members, the branch is their main contact with the union and the key point at which collective action could make a difference to their working lives. The focus of much self-organisation, however, has been at regional level. It is here that women have been encouraged to attend innovative forums and have taken part in informative workshops and educational activities. Back at the branch, women have experienced difficulties setting up self-organised groups. Some have faced resistance from their male colleagues and others have found it hard to attract women participants. Some women have no contact with their union at branch level – and most regional self-organised groups would not expect this. The need to organise oppressed social groups at a local level is accepted within UNISON (see also Colgan, 2000). The most appropriate form, however, needs to be explored. Is it more effective to organise around women shop stewards than all women members? This is an important question, as research indicates that the concerns of women, as a group, are not being met at branch level (Munro, 1999; Conley, 2000; Waddington and Kerr, 2000).

Briskin (1999) indicates that the discourse for describing and discussing women's organizing has not always kept pace with the developments themselves. In recording two different approaches to organising women, this study reminds us that terms used in this literature such as self-organisation, women-only structures, separate organising and group representation require constant refinement. Briskin notes that 'self-organisation' is Colgan and Ledwith's (1998) term for 'separate organizing'. Given that the organisation of women shop stewards fits more easily into the latter category than the former, it would be useful to revisit the assumptions underpinning these terms and develop a typology covering the range of activities within women-only organisations.

The implications of new sources of power for women

So, what is to be learnt from this extensive case study of UNISON? What do the interviews, non-participant observation of committee meetings and document examination tell us? They tell us that UNISON has managed to reshape the traditional model of trade union democracy. They provide illustrations of how women are pushed and pulled into decision-making arenas. Once there, women learn new skills of representation and participation. Their explicit inclusion in the democratic process means individual women shape arguments outside and inside meetings. This change in political processes has provided opportunities for gender to be made more visible and male norms to be challenged. Women are speaking for women and some issues are subject to a gendered analysis.

In essence, this study tells us that principles of proportionality and fair representation do make a difference to representation by individual women in the union.

However, the inclusion of individual women does not guarantee that women as a group have a stronger voice in the union. Detailed observation of mixed sex and women-only meetings reveal that the concerns of women as a group are not necessarily pursued at committee level. This is underpinned by two dynamics. The first, that too much emphasis is placed on individual women to push women's concerns. The second, that insufficient attention has been paid to empowering self-organised groups in relation to those privileged groups holding formal power.

I believe three key issues emerge from UNISON's radical attempts to reshape traditional models of trade union democracy. First, UNISON has shown that it is possible to reshape structures so characteristics of representatives more closely mirror the characteristics of constituents. In this respect UNISON has developed a structure that provides for basic justice to be achieved for women. Second, representation by individual women does not guarantee the representation of women as a group. Third, supporting women's self-organisation is not the same as providing rights of representation to women as a group. These issues have two implications for unions and other political institutions serious about providing women and other oppressed groups with a voice.

The first implication is for the majority of unions and political organisations that do not provide mechanisms for mirror representation. This study has shown that constitutions can support the election of individual women in proportion to their membership. A first step is a commitment to change the balance of power between different constituencies. UNISON was committed to change from the beginning of the merger process. This commitment, embedded in the first rule book, has been an important factor in enabling women's representation of UNISON to be significantly different to that in the former partner unions. Turning this commitment into reality requires the identification of specific groups of constituents, the categorisation of seats and the use of multi-representative constituencies. Organisations need to prove their commitment to fair representation by addressing the exclusive nature of their representative structures.

The second implication is for those unions already tackling the under-representation of women. This study has tried to show that the representation of women as a group requires a more radical reshaping of union democracy than that originally proposed in UNISON's rule book. UNISON has started along the route of providing rights of representation to groups, in addition to individuals. If unions and other political institutions are serious about providing women, and other oppressed groups, with a stronger voice, they too need to consider the collective advantages of group representation.

Appendix

Schedule of research themes and data collection

Theme 1: Women gaining access through proportionality and fair representation

Research sites

National Executive Council (NEC)
Local Government Service Group Executive (LGSGE)
Health Care Service Group Executive (HCSGE)
Regional Committee (Region 1) (RC1)
Regional Committee (Region 2) (RC2)

Data collection and research methods

Documentation in relation to all of above research sites:
Committee structures; election addresses; election results; Minutes and Agenda.

1–2 hour semi-structured interviews with candidates standing for elections, members and paid officers servicing the committees:
7 candidates NEC; 4 candidates LGSGE; 1 paid officer LGSGE; 2 candidates HCSGE; 1 paid officer HCSGE; 4 candidates RC1; 2 paid officers RC1; 7 candidates RC2; 2 paid officers RC2.

Non-participant observation of following meetings when structure and elections discussed:
3 meetings of HCSGE (1 day each); 1 HCSG Conference (2 days); 2 meetings in RC2 (1 day each).

Theme 2: Creating a separate space for women through self-organisation

Research sites

National Women's Committee (NWC)
National Women's Conference
Women-only structures (Region 1)
Women-only structures (Region 2)

Data collection and research methods

Documentation in relation to the above research sites:
Committee structures; election addresses; election results; Minutes and Agenda of relevant Committees and Conferences.

1–2 hour semi-structured interviews with members of above committees and paid officers servicing the committees:
5 members NWC; 2 national paid officers; 6 members Region 1; 1 paid officer Region 1; 2 members Region 2; 1 paid officer Region 2.

Non-participant observation of meetings of above committees:
5 meetings NWC (1–2 days each); 1995 National Women's Conference (2 days); 1 meeting of National Standing Committee for 1995 Women's Conference (2 days); 1995 Women's TUC Conference with informal discussions with UNISON delegation over 2 days; 5 meetings Region 1 (half-day each); 1994 and 1995; Women's Forum (Region 1) (1 day each); 4 meetings Region 2 (half-day each).

Participant observation of:
1-day seminar for Regional Women's Officers; two 2-day educational activities organised by Women-only structure (Region 2); two public demonstrations against public sector cuts.

Questionnaire completed by:
17 participants at 1994 Women's Forum (Region 1)
24 participants at 1995 Women's Forum (Region 1)

Theme 3: Impact of three principles on content of decision-making arenas

Research sites

Regional Committee (Region 2); Local Government Service Group Executive; National Delegate Conference (NDC).

Data collection and research methods

Documentation in relation to all of above research sites:
Minutes and Agenda of Committees and relevant Conferences; 1994, 1995 UNISON Annual Reports.

1–2 hours semi-structured interviews with members of above committees and paid officers servicing the committees:
10 members RC2; 2 paid officers RC2; 4 members LGSGE; 10 members of Local Government Service Group active at branch or regional level; 3 national paid officers; 1 regional paid officer.

Non-participant observation of meetings of above committees:
4 Regional Committee (1 day each); 4 Regional Council (1 day each); 5 LGSGE (1–2 days each); 1 2-day LGSG Conference; 3 Regional Local Government Committee (Region 1) (half-day each); 1994 and 1995 National Delegate Conference (3 days each).

I conducted formal interviews with 38 individuals, 25 of whom were representatives and 13 were paid officers. The higher number of interviews recorded above (77) reflects two factors: (i) 14 interviewees provided information for themes 1 and 2 and have been 'double-counted', (ii) a number of UNISON representatives operate simultaneously at different levels within the union. For example, some women are involved in the regional women's structures and the national mainstream structures. Of the 25 representatives I interviewed, 22 were women. Of the 13 officers I interviewed, nine were women. Virtually all representatives in mainstream and women-only committees were white. Consequently, only one of my interviewees was black. I attended a total of 64 meetings and activities during my research. I spoke informally to many representatives and members on these occasions, often during breaks, over lunch or leaving buildings. On occasion, I travelled to and from these meetings with representatives. Of particular importance are the informal women-only activities I attended. Significantly more black women were involved in these activities, enabling me to speak, and listen, to a greater number of black women members.

Bibliography

Bachrach, P. and Baratz, M. (1970), *Power and Poverty: Theory and Practice*, Oxford University Press, New York.

Batstone, E., Boraston, I., and Frenkel, S. (1979), *Shop Stewards in Action: The Organisation of Workplace Conflict and Accommodation*, Blackwell, Oxford.

Beale, J. (1982), *Getting it together: Women as Trade Unionists*, Pluto Press, London.

Bradley, H. (1999), *Gender and Power in the Workplace*, Macmillan, Basingstoke.

Briskin, L. (1993), 'Union Women and Separate Organizing' in Briskin and McDermott (eds), *Women Challenging Unions*, University of Toronto Press, Toronto.

Briskin, L. (1999), 'Autonomy, Diversity, and Integration: Union Women's Separate Organizing in North America and Western Europe in the Context of Restructuring and Globalization', *Women's Studies International Forum*, Vol. 22(5), pp. 543–54.

Briskin, L. and McDermott, P. (eds) (1993a), *Women Challenging Unions*, University of Toronto Press, Toronto.

Briskin, L. and McDermott, P. (1993b), 'The Feminist Challenge to the Unions' in L. Briskin and P. McDermott (eds), *Women Challenging Unions*, University of Toronto Press, Toronto.

Carpenter, M. (1988), *Working for Health The History of COHSE*, Lawrence & Wishart, London.

Cobble, D.S. (1990), 'Rethinking Troubled Relations between Women and Unions: Craft Unionism and Female Activism', *Feminist Studies*, vol. 16(3), pp. 519–48.

Cockburn, C. (1983), *Brothers: Male Dominance and Technological Change*, Pluto Press, London.

Cockburn, C. (1989), 'Equal Opportunities: The Short and Long Agenda', *Industrial Relations Journal*, vol. 20(3), pp. 213–25.

Cockburn, C. (1991), *In the Way of Women*, Macmillan, London.

Cockburn, C. (1996), *Strategies for Gender Democracy: Women and the European Social Dialogue*, European Commission, Employment, Industrial Relations and Social Affairs, Supplement 4, 95.

COHSE, NALGO, NUPE (1990), *The Challenge of a new Union: report to Annual Conferences*.

COHSE, NALGO, NUPE (1991), *A Framework for a New Union: report to Annual Conferences*.

COHSE, NALGO, NUPE (1992), *Towards a New Union, report to special conference*.

Colgan, F. (2000), 'Recognising the lesbian and gay constituency in UK trade unions: moving forward in UNISON?', *Industrial Relations Journal*, vol. 30(5), pp. 444–63.

Colgan, F. and Ledwith, S. (1996), 'Sisters Organising – Women and Their Trade Unions' in S. Ledwith and F. Colgan (eds), *Women in Organisations – Challenging Gender Politics*, Macmillan, Basingstoke.

Colgan, F. and Ledwith, S. (2000), 'Diversity, Identities and Strategies of women trade union activists', *Gender, Work and Organization*, vol. 7(4), pp. 242–57.

Colling, T. (1995), 'Renewal or Rigor Mortis? Union Responses to Contracting in Local Government', *Industrial Relations Journal* vol. 26(2), pp. 134–45.

Colling, T. and Dickens, L. (1989), *Equality Bargaining – Why not?*, Industrial Relations Research Unit, University of Warwick, Coventry.

Conley, H. (2000) 'Temporary Work and Temporary Members: Representing the Insecure Workforce in the Public Sector', paper presented at the British Universities Industrial Relations Association Conference, University of Warwick, 7-9 July 2000.

Cunnison, S. and Stageman, J. (1993), *Feminizing the Unions*, Avebury, Aldershot.

Cyba, E. and Papouschek, U. (1996), 'Women's interests in the Workplace. Between delegation and self-representation', *Transfer*, 1, pp. 61–81.

Dix, B. and Williams, S. (1987), *Serving the Public – Building the Union: The History of NUPE*, Lawrence & Wishart, London.

Edelstein, J.D. (1967), 'An Organizational Theory of Union Democracy', *American Sociological Review*, vol. 32, pp. 19–39.

Escott, K. and Whitfield, D. (1995), *The Gender Impact of CCT in Local Government*, Equal Opportunities Commission, Manchester.

Fairbrother, P. (1984), *All those in Favour: The Politics of Union Democracy*, Pluto Press, London.

Fairbrother, P. (1996), 'Workplace Trade Unionism in the State Sector', in P. Ackers, C. Smith, and P. Smith (eds), *The New Workplace and Trade Unionism*, Routledge, London.

Fryer, R. (2000), 'Form and Character in the Making of UNISON', in M. Terry, (ed.), *Redefining Public Sector Unionism: UNISON and the future of Trade Unions*, Routledge, London.

Fryer, R., Fairclough, A., and Manson, T. (1974), *Organisation and Change in NUPE*, Department of Sociology, University of Warwick, Coventry.

Fryer, R.H., Fairclough, A.J., and Manson, T.B. (1978), 'Facilities for Female Shop Stewards: The Employment Protection Act and Collective Agreements', *British Journal of Industrial Relations* vol. 16(2), pp. 160–74.

Gouldner, A. (1955), 'Metaphysical pathos and the theory of bureaucracy', *American Political Science Review*, vol. 49(2), pp. 496-507.

Harlow, E., Hearn, J., and Parkin, W. (1995) 'Gendered Noise: organizations and the silence and din of domination', in C. Itzin and J. Newman (eds), *Gender, Culture and Organizational Change*, Routledge, London.

Hastings, S. (1995), 'Single Status Employment for Local Government Employees: A review for the Trade Union Side of the Options', unpublished paper written for UNISON.

Heery, E. and Kelly, J. (1988a), 'Do female representatives make a difference? Women Full-time Officials and trade union work', *Work, Employment and Society*, vol. 2(4), pp. 487–505.

Heery, E. and Kelly, J. (1988b) *A Study of Women Trade Union Officers*, London School of Economics, London.

Heery, E. and Kelly, J. (1989), '"A cracking job for a woman" – a profile of women trade union officers', *Industrial Relations Journal*, vol. 20(3), pp. 192-202.

Hicks, S. (2000), 'Trade union membership 1998–99: an analysis of data from the Certification Officer and Labour Force Survey', *Labour Market Trends*, vol. 108(7), pp. 329–40.

Higgins, W. (1996), 'The Swedish Municipal Workers' Union – A study in the New Political Unionism', *Economic and Industrial Democracy*, vol. 17, pp. 167–97.

Holden, B. (1993), *Understanding Liberal Democracy*, Harvester Wheatsheaf, Hemel Hempstead.

Hyman, R. (1971a), *Marxism and the Sociology of Trade Unionism*, Pluto Press, London.

Hyman, R. (1971b), *The Workers' Union*, Clarendon Press, Oxford.

Hyman, R. (1975), *Industrial Relations: A Marxist Introduction*, Macmillan, London.

Hyman, R. (1989), *The Political Economy of Industrial Relations: Theory and Practice in a Cold Climate*, Macmillan, Basingstoke.

Hyman, R. (1997), 'Trade Unions and interest representation in the context of Globalisation', *Transfer*, vol. 3(3), pp. 515–33.

IRS (1998), 'Goodbye CCT', *IRS Employment Trends*, January, pp. 5–11.

James, L. (1984) *Power in a Trade Union*, Cambridge University Press, Cambridge.

Jones, M. (2000), 'Working with Labour: the impact of UNISON's political settlement' in M. Terry (ed.), *Redefining Public Sector Unionism: UNISON and the future of Trade Unions*, Routledge, London.

Kealey, H. (1990), 'What Union Women Want: The Involvement and Representation of Women in COHSE, NALGO and NUPE', unpublished Masters dissertation, University of Warwick, Coventry.

Kelly, J. (1998), *Rethinking Industrial Relations*, Routledge, London.

Kelly, J. and Heery, E. (1994), *Working for the Union: British Trade Union Officers*, Cambridge University Press, Cambridge.

Labour Research (1993), 'Public Service Workers Unite!', *Labour Research*, January, pp. 11–12.

Labour Research (1994), 'Still a long road to equality', *Labour Research*, March, pp. 5–7.

Labour Research (1999), 'The municipal pressure cooker', *Labour Research*, November, pp. 19–20.

Labour Research (2000), 'Women everywhere but the top', *Labour Research*, March, pp. 17–19.

Lane, T. (1974), *The Union Makes Us Strong*, Arrow, London.

Lawrence, E. (1994), *Gender and Trade Unions*, Taylor & Francis, London.

Ledwith, S. and Colgan, F. (eds) (1996), *Women in Organisations – Challenging Gender Politics*, Macmillan, Basingstoke.

Leidner, R. (1991), 'Stretching the Boundaries of Liberalism: Democracy Innovation in a Feminist Organization', *Signs: Journal of Women in Culture and Society*, vol. 16(21), pp. 263–89.

Lipset, S.M., Trow, M.A., and Coleman, J.S. (1956), *Union Democracy*, Free Press, Glencoe, Illinois.

Lukes, S. (1974), *Power – A Radical View*, Macmillan, London.

Martin, R. (1968), 'Union Democracy: An Explanatory Framework', *Sociology*, vol. 2, pp. 205–20.

McBride, A. (1997), 'Re-shaping Trade Union Democracy: Developing Effective Representation for women in UNISON', unpublished PhD Thesis, University of Warwick, Coventry.

Michels, R. (1915), *Political Parties*, 2nd Edn., Free Press, New York.

Miller, C. (1996), *Public Service Trade Unionism and Radical Politics*, Dartmouth, Aldershot.

Millward, N., Bryson, A., and Forth, J. (2000), *All Change at Work? British employment relations 1980 – 1998, as portrayed by the Workplace Industrial Relations series*, Routledge, London.

Munro, A. (1999), *Women, Work and Trade Unions*, Mansell, London.

Newman, G. (1982), *Path to Maturity: NALGO 1965–80*, NALGO, London.

Nightingale, M. (1991), *Facing the Challenge*, Victorian Trades Hall Council, Melbourne.

Ouroussoff, A. (1993), 'UNISON: Building a New Culture', unpublished paper written for UNISON.

Park, T. (1999), 'In and Beyond the Workplace: the search for articulated trade unionism in UNISON', unpublished PhD thesis, University of Warwick, Coventry.

Pateman, C. (1970), *Participation and Democratic Theory*, Cambridge University Press, London.

Pateman, C (1983), 'Some reflections on *Participation and Democratic Theory*' in C. Crouch and F. Heller (eds), *Organisational Democracy and Political Processes*, Wiley, Chichester.

Pateman, C. (1988), *The Sexual Contract*, Polity Press, Cambridge.

Phillips, A. (1991), *Engendering Democracy*, Polity Press, Cambridge.

Phillips, A. (1993), *Democracy and Difference*, Polity Press, Cambridge.

Phillips, A. (1999), *Which Equalities Matter*, Polity Press, Cambridge.

Sartori, G. (1965) *Democratic Theory*, Praeger, New York.

Sartori, G. (1987) *The Theory of Democracy Revisited*, 2 vols., Chatham House, Chatham.

Schattschneider, E.E., (1960), *The Semi-Sovereign People: A Realist's View of Democracy in America*, Holt, Rinehart & Winston, New York.

Short, E. (1995), 'Proportionality: no way forward for women workers', *Socialist Appeal*, June 1995 UNISON Conference Special.

Southern and Eastern Regional TUC Women's Rights Committee (1997), *Inching* towards equality, *extremely slowly*, Southern & Eastern Region TUC, London.

Southern and Eastern Regional TUC Women's Rights Committee (2000), *New moves towards equality*, Southern & Eastern Region TUC, London.

Spoor, A. (1967), *White Collar Union: Sixty years of NALGO*, Heinemann, London.

Terry, M. (1996), 'Negotiating the Government of Unison: Union Democracy in Theory and Practice', *British Journal of Industrial Relations*, vol. 34, pp. 87–110.

Terry, M. (ed.) (2000), *Redefining Public Sector Unionism: UNISON and the future of Trade Unions*, Routledge, London.

Trebilcock, A. (1991), 'Strategies for Strengthening Women's Participation in Trade Union Leadership', *International Labour Review*, vol. 130(4), pp. 407-26.

Trades Union Congress (1999), *The Directory*, TUC, London.

UNISON (1993), *Rules as at Vesting Day*, UNISON, London.

UNISON (1994a), *UNISON rules as amended at the 1994 Conference*, UNISON, London.

UNISON (1994b), *Code of Good Branch Practice*, UNISON, London.

UNISON (1994c), *Getting the Balance Right: Guidelines on Proportionality*, UNISON, London.

UNISON (1994d), *Quality Counts: Dealing with White Collar Compulsory Competitive Tendering*, UNISON, London.

UNISON (1994e), *Conference Guide, UNISON First National Delegate Conference*, UNISON, London.

UNISON (1994f), *National Women's Committee Report*, UNISON, London.

UNISON (1995a), *Integration and Participation in UNISON: From Vision to Practice*, Report of the Joint Working Group, 1995, UNISON, London.

UNISON (1995b), *Retendering Guide: CCT in Manual Services*, UNISON, London.

UNISON (1995c), *Conference Guide, UNISON Second National Delegate Conference*, UNISON, London.

UNISON (1996a), *Conference Guide, UNISON Third National Delegate Conference*, UNISON, London.

UNISON (1996b), *Single Status – a national agreement for the future – briefing for UNISON branches and regions*, UNISON, London.

UNISON (1997a), *UNISON rules As amended at the 1997 Conference*, UNISON, London.

UNISON (1997b), *Playing fair, UNISON guidelines on fair representation*, UNISON, London.

UNISON (1998a), *Get yourself organised, UNISON guidelines on self organisation*, UNISON, London.

UNISON (1998b), *Women, Work & UNISON, first report of the Women's Development Project*, UNISON, London.

UNISON (2000), *UNISON rules as amended at the 2000 Conference*, UNISON, London.

Virdie, S. and Grint, K. (1994), 'Black Self-organisation in Trade Unions', *Sociological Review*, vol. 42(2), pp. 202–26.

Waddington, J. and Kerr, A. (2000), 'Towards an organising model in UNISON?: a trade union membership strategy in transition', in Terry, M. (ed.), *Redefining Public Sector Unionism: UNISON and the future of Trade Unions*, Routledge, London.

Waddington, J. and Whitston, C. (1995), 'Trade Unions: Growth, Structure and Policy', in P. Edwards (ed.), *Industrial Relations: Theory and Practice in Britain*, Blackwell, Oxford.

Wheeler, M. (2000), 'UNISON's approach to organisation development in a democratic organisation' in M. Terry, (ed.), *Redefining Public Sector Unionism: UNISON and the future of Trade Unions*, Routledge, London.

Young, I.M. (1990), *Justice and the Politics of Difference*, Princeton University Press, Princeton.

QUEEN MARY
UNIVERSITY OF LONDON
LIBRARY